P9-CCV-764

PAUL RICOEUR

Charles E. Reagan

PAUL RICOEUR
His Life and His Work

The University of Chicago Press
CHICAGO & LONDON

Charles E. Reagan is executive assistant to the president of Kansas State University. From 1967 to 1986 he was professor and head of the Department of Philosophy of Kansas State University.

THE UNIVERSITY OF CHICAGO PRESS, CHICAGO 60637
THE UNIVERSITY OF CHICAGO PRESS, LTD., LONDON

© 1996 by The University of Chicago
All rights reserved. Published 1996

Printed in the United States of America

05 04 03 02 01 00 99 98 97 96   1 2 3 4 5

ISBN 0–226–70602–8

Library of Congress Cataloging-in-Publication Data

Reagan, Charles E.
    Paul Ricoeur : his life and his work / Charles E. Reagan.
        p.   cm.
    Includes bibliographical references and index.
    1. Ricoeur, Paul.   I. Title.
    B2430.R554R43   1996
    194—dc20
    [B]   95-52099

⊗ The paper used in this publication meets the minimum requirements of the American National Standard for Information Sciences—Permanence of Paper for Printed Library Materials, ANSI Z39.48–1984

To my wife, Sharon, and my late friend, Olivier

CONTENTS

ACKNOWLEDGMENTS ix

INTRODUCTION 1

•1•

BIOGRAPHICAL ESSAY 4

•2•

MEMOIR 52

•3•

PHILOSOPHICAL ESSAY 73

•4•

INTERVIEWS 100

June 19, 1982, Chatenay-Malabry 100
October 26, 1988, Chicago 009
May 17, 1990, Chicago 116
July 8, 1991, Chatenay-Malabry 123

BIBLIOGRAPHY 137

INDEX 147

A group of photos follows p. 54 and p. 118.

ACKNOWLEDGMENTS

THE AUTHOR of any work of this complexity owes many people his heartfelt gratitude. First, and foremost, I want to express my deepest appreciation to Paul and Simone Ricoeur. I will never forget the kindness, hospitality, and affection they have given my wife, Sharon, and me and our family. I also want to thank all of the Ricoeur children for their help. I will never forget my friend, Olivier Ricoeur, and all of the friendship and help he gave us. I owe a real debt to my friend and colleague, David Stewart, my intellectual and sometime traveling companion, whose constant encouragement kept me on-task. I thank Elizabeth Roudinesco for her friendship and encouragement. I want also to thank Olivier Abel, David Pellauer, Kit Blamey, Therese DuFlot, David Tracy, Gerald Brauer, Andre and Claire Lacocque, Betty McGraw, William Richter, and Andrew McKenna for the many ways they helped advance this project.

I especially appreciate those individuals at Kansas State University who provided financial support and encouragement over a long period of time. In particular, Dean Robert Kruh and Dean William Stamey were very supportive. President Jon Wefald gave me encouragement, time, and the travel funds to complete the research and the manuscript. Special appreciation to my secretary, Dana Hastings, who helped put the manuscript in final order.

This project took many years to complete. During this time, there were many skeptics who doubted I would ever finish it. So, I feel special love and appreciation for my wife, Sharon, who never doubted, always encouraged, and shared many of the experiences I recount in this book.

INTRODUCTION

"Genres are not to be mixed. I will not mix genres."
—Jacques Derrida

T HIS BOOK is precisely a mix of genres. The first chapter is a biographical essay, not a biography as a historian would write it. It lacks the detail, the intense documentation, and the proper "distance" of a true history. The second chapter is even more personal; it is a memoir of Paul Ricoeur as told by a student who became his friend; a friend whom he invited to live in his house and know his family; a friend who became a confidant. So my memoir seeks to paint a portrait of a philosopher, an "acting and suffering human"; at the same time, I intend to exercise the responsibility of a confidant. This requirement, in particular, forces me to run a risk. How much needs to be said? How much am I permitted to say? If I must offend, my principle is to offend the reader who may want to know more, rather than to offend my friend. There is another time . . . and another author of a complete history, if such is wanted or if such is warranted. The third chapter is a philosophical essay, not an argument for a particular point in a philosophical debate, not an explanation of a difficult text, not even a critique of the arguments. Rather, it is an essay with the dual goals of showing Ricoeur's philosophical style and some of his main points. But, more important, it is a tribute to a professor by way of what one of his students has learned about philosophy from him.

Finally, I contribute four unpublished interviews with Paul Ricoeur which I made over the course of ten years. These interviews let Paul speak with his own voice to the questions that occupied us at various periods over a long friendship. They are mostly about his philosophical works and interests at the time. I am especially pleased with the last one, which is much more personal than the preceding three.

When I began this project, in 1980, Paul told me two things: "No one is interested in my life," and "My life is my work, I mean, my books and my articles." I disagree with both of these claims, although the latter is closer to the truth than the former. This is why the biographical essay is marked, cadenced even, with the articles and the books that gained for Paul Ricoeur the acclaim he has received. There is no doubt that intellectual pursuits, from his school days to the prolific publications of his "retirement," are at the center of his life. Even his five years as a prisoner of war in Germany are principally remembered as years of reading, years of writing drafts for later books, and as years of preparing and giving courses.

To the extent that Paul is right, there are others, many others, who can do and have done a better job than I in explaining his philosophical positions and theses, critiquing his claims, and analyzing his arguments. This is why, in this book, I have abandoned the ambition to give a careful and thorough exposition and critique of each of his books and principal articles. In the bibliography I refer the reader to the best of those expositions.

The biographical essay is based on conversations with Paul and Simone Ricoeur, but is is supported by independent evidence appropriate to a historian, such as interviews, books, newspaper articles, published works, and so forth. My goal has not been an exhaustive history but a credible one. In the memoir, I base my descriptions on my personal experience, my notes on conversations with the Ricoeurs over the years, and my conversations with others. There are many other close friends and colleagues of Paul and Simone Ricoeur who could—and, I hope, will—contribute their memoirs, at other times, and in other ways, to the "historical record" of this remarkable man.

From the point of view of everyday life, Paul Ricoeur seems to have led the most ordinary of lives: intellectual work of reading, writing, teaching, lecturing; domestic life of marriage, children, grandchildren. He traveled extensively to give lectures, for vacations, to tour. But this "ordinary life" masks an extraordinary life, unusual in many ways. For example, Ricoeur's life has been a continual contradiction between his pacifism and his direct and indirect involvement in war. He was orphaned by one war, imprisoned during another, and a leader of the opposition to yet another war. His devotion to the peaceful resolution of conflicts through reason and good will was severely challenged by his experience as the Doyen at the University of Paris-Nanterre. This is why certain of his experiences are treated in greater depth in this biography. They were not only important periods in his life, but they had an enduring influence on his philosophy.

Let me finish this Introduction by explaining an existential decision: In this book, both in the biography and the memoir, I will say very little of Paul and Simone's children and grand-children. They are very important to Paul and Simone, but not essential to my goal in this book. Nevertheless, I will write about Olivier, Paul and Simone's fourth child, and my close friend. It is a tragic story, and I debated long and hard on what and how much to include. Paul dedicates an "Interlude" in *Oneself as Another* to Olivier because his suicide has left an indelible mark on his parents and friends. Paul and Simone's other children have a right to their privacy and Paul's story can be told without telling their stories.

So, if there was ever a case of "mixing genres," this book is a perfect example,

2

but the subject of the book exceeds the bounds of a single genre. Yet, there is an underlying unity. The "voices" and the genres change with each chapter, but the goal is to answer—in Ricoeur's own style—four questions about Paul Ricoeur and his work: What has he done? (biographical essay); What kind of person is he? (memoir); What has he said about the self and its relation with others—and what has he taught his students about doing philosophy? (philosophical essay); What does he say about his own work during his most prolific period? (interviews). This book is, in no way, a complete answer to these questions, but it can serve as an introduction to the life and work of Paul Ricoeur.

BIOGRAPHICAL ESSAY

The Early Years

J EAN PAUL GUSTAVE RICOEUR was born on February 27, 1913, at Valence, a small city of 25,000 in habitants some 42 kilometers south of Lyons. His father, Jules Ricoeur, originally from Normandy, was a professor of English at the lycée. Valence is the administrative city of the Department of la Drôme and has textiles, metals, and munitions as its principal industries. Very little is known about Paul's mother, Florentine Favre, who died in September of 1913 when Paul was only seven months old.

Paul and his sister, Alice, born two years before him, lived with their father until he was mobilized for World War I. They then went to live with Jules' parents and sister, Adèle, in Rennes. On September 26, 1915, Jules Ricoeur was declared missing in action and presumed dead in the Battle of the Marne. His remains were later found. So Paul and Alice were raised by their paternal grandparents, Louis and Marie Ricoeur. Their home in Rennes was a relatively large apartment in a three-story white building on Rue de Sévigné, only a short distance north of the University of Rennes.

The Ricoeurs were very devout Protestants, and Paul was raised in a strict atmosphere of reading, Bible study, and going to church. When he went out to play, it was under the close supervision of his grandmother or his aunt, Adèle. She was twenty years older than Paul and much of the role of mothering fell to her. The main disciplinary tool was the reproach, "But Paul, what would your father say about that if he were here?"

As a "Pupille de la Nation" (literally, "orphan of the state"), Paul received from the government a small stipend each year to buy books and to pay other school expenses. This was a right of every child whose father had been killed in the Great War. Paul would buy all of the books for the next year at the beginning of the summer. He would then spend much of his time, especially on rainy days, reading the textbooks. This habit had two consequences: he found himself bored during the school year since he had already done most of the work; and he still spends his summer vacations in the same way, largely in reading and writing. Like many bright but bored youngsters, he played pranks and occasionally misbehaved. On the other hand, he was always far ahead of other children and did a great deal of additional reading. His years in primary school and the lycée (high school) followed this regular pattern and passed uneventfully.

In 1928, Paul's grandmother died and his aunt took charge of him and his sister, Alice. Alice was slender and frail and always took second place in the family after Paul. But Paul was very attached to his older sister, who was his confidante and friend. Alice's good friend was Simone Lejas, whom Paul met for the first time when he was eight years old. The three of them were involved in scouting and were seen everywhere together. On April 20, 1931, Paul and Simone were engaged to be married.

Two years later, in 1933, two significant events occurred: Paul's grandfather died, and Paul received his *Licence-ès-Lettres* from the University of Rennes. At the university, Paul was an outstanding student. In those days, even more than today, Paris was the intellectual center of France, and the provincial universities were rather weak. Paul had spent the first two years at the University of Rennes preparing for the competitive examination for entrance to the prestigious Ecole normale supérieure in Paris. He did very well on the Latin and Greek parts of the exam, but, ironically, he failed the philosophy section. The question was, "The mind is easier to know than the body." Paul did not recognize this as a thesis of Descartes' and gave the Aristotelian answer to it which he had learned from his provincial professors.

Still, there were some exceptional professors in Rennes. Roland Dalbiez was one of Paul's professors at the lycée who had a positive influence on him. Paul had always wanted to be a professor. He was extremely good at Greek and Latin and planned to pursue graduate studies in classical languages. In fact, Paul had shied away from philosophy. Perhaps he thought it would be a threat to his devotion to religion. In any case, it was Dalbiez, a professor of philosophy, who told Paul that whenever he was afraid of something, he should go directly at it. So Paul began to study philosophy and later chose it as his life's work.

The university degree of "license" was then literally a license to teach. So, in the fall of that year, Paul took a position of professor of philosophy at the lycée in St. Brieuc, a small fishing town on the north cost of Brittany, about 100 kilometers northwest of Rennes. He continued his reading in philosophy and, of course, his frequent visits to Rennes to see Simone and his sister, who was suffering from tuberculosis.

A year later, in the fall of 1934, Paul enrolled at the Sorbonne to study for the *agrégation*, a competitive examination which gave those who were "received" (successful) the right to serve as an examiner for the *baccalauréat*. The examination was also expected of anyone who hoped to move up from the lycée to the university. He received a small fellowship, once again, as a Pupille de la Nation.

During this same period, Paul was bereaved again, this time by the death of his dear sister who succumbed to her illness. She had been courageous and bore her suffering patiently. Paul and Simone visited her frequently and were grieved by their loss.

Summer vacation was spent in a very small house at Préfailles, near Pornic, about 50 kilometers south of Nantes, on the coast of Britanny. The house was several streets back from the coast itself, but numerous small beaches were nearby, as were the paths along the rocky coast which Paul loved to walk. This house, now expanded, has been the focal point of family gatherings, and the retreat to which Paul has come every summer and whenever he needed space and time to think during other parts of the year.

During his year of studies at the Sorbonne, Paul met the philosopher Gabriel Marcel, who would later have a great influence on him personally and on his work. On August 5, 1935, Paul was notified that he was second in the *agrégation*. This is a very strenuous series of written and oral examinations. The results are competitive: since receiving the *agrégation* means that a person is guaranteed a teaching position in France, the number of successful candidates exactly equals the number of vacant positions, no matter how many take the examination. The year that Paul was successful there were three hundred who took the examination, and only ten were received. With this significant achievement in hand— and the security of knowing he had a job—Paul and Simone were married in Rennes. But if the *agrégation* guarantees one a position, it does not give the right to choose where. So Paul and Simone went to Colmar, a city in the Alsace, about 70 kilometers south of Strasbourg, on the French-German border. He was professor of philosophy at the lycée.

At the end of that year, Simone returned to Rennes, while Paul did his year of obligatory military service. He was first sent to the military school at St. Cyr, just outside of Versailles, southwest of Paris. This was an officer candidate school where reserve officers received their training. He was later sent to finish his year at a military barrack in Rennes, where he was commissioned a reserve lieutenant. It was during this period, on January 15, 1937, that their first child was born, a son, Jean-Paul.

Paul was able to get a teaching assignment closer to home for the next two years. He taught philosophy at the lycée in Lorient, a city on the southwest coast of Brittany, approximately 160 kilometers southwest of Rennes. On February 22, 1938, their second son, Marc, was born.

During this period, from 1935 to 1940, Ricoeur began his long and prolific career as an author. His writings were mostly arguments for Christian socialism and pacifism. Some of the titles were: "Arms merchants," "Short thesis of a young philosopher: Christianity by way of socialism," "A plea for disarmament,"

"Workers should only defend a republic of workers," "Resist in order to govern," "Where is France going? A loss of speed," and "For a constructive socialism." These were short texts published in a regional review.[1] In 1940, he published his first paper with "phenomenology" in the title: "Attention: A phenomenological study of attention and its philosophical connections."[2] This was his last publication until after the war.

In August of 1939 Paul received a small grant to go to Munich to perfect his German. Simone went with him, leaving their two small boys with Simone's parents at the summer cottage in Préfailles. About halfway through the six-week course, they saw large billboard signs being put up all over Munich announcing the German-Soviet Nonaggression Pact. Simone was convinced that war was near. Paul, however, was very reluctant to leave before the end of the course. To settle the disagreement over whether they should stay or go, they went together to the French consulate in Munich. The consul was aghast that there were still French citizens in Germany and urged them to leave at once. They packed to leave, but they could not find Paul's passport. A great hunt began, with their landlady helping them search every inch of their room, but they could not find the passport. Finally, they remembered that when they arrived they had changed money at the bank at the train station. They went there and, with great relief, found his passport posted up in the window. So they took the next train to France.

The War Years

ON SEPTEMBER 3, 1939, Britain and France declared war on Germany as a result of the German invasion of Poland. France immediately mobilized its armed forces and Paul was called to active military service with his regiment of Bretons. His regiment was the 47th Infantry with barracks at St. Malo, an ancient walled port about 70 kilometers north of Rennes, on the north coast of Brittany. It was a difficult and boring year. They had only old equipment and the training was half-hearted. The French call it the *drôle de guerre,* the period of calm before the storm. Feelings of pacifism and noninterventionism were strong in France at that time, and Paul certainly shared them.

Simone spent the year of mobilization in Rennes, with Jean-Paul and Marc. Paul was granted occasional leaves and would make the short trip to Rennes to visit them. He missed his teaching, his family, and he was opposed to war.

On May 10, 1940, the Germans began their invasion of France. Belgium had capitulated and the British were driven off the Continent at Dunkirk. Paul's unit was sent to the Marne valley, near Reims. By early June, the Germans had by-

1. These and other brief articles and book reviews were published in the journal *Terre nouvelle.*
2. Paul Ricoeur, "L'attention. Étude phénoménologique de l'attention et de ses connexions philosophiques," *Bulletin du Cercle philosophique de l'Ouest* 4 (1940) January-March, 1–28.

passed them and had already entered Paris. The Bretons continued fighting until they were surrounded and forced to surrender. Paul was captured at Dormans, a small village near Chateau Thierry, some 60 kilometers southwest of Reims. In spite of his strong feelings of pacifism, he was a good soldier, even blowing up a bridge with a German tank on it. He received the Croix de Guerre with three palm leaves, but he never wore it and never spoke about it.

The most remarkable thing that happened to him during his short war occurred when he was standing next to his captain, a close friend of his from Rennes, when the captain took a bullet in the head and was killed instantly. Paul realized that it could have just as easily been him in the sights of the sniper. He could have met the same fate—in almost the same place—as his father had met some twenty-six years before. From that moment on, he never took living for granted.

On June 7, 1940, Paul became a prisoner of war and would remain one for almost five full years. The French prisoners were marched to a railhead over a period of days. They were fed at most once a day. The enlisted men were separated from the officers and the two groups were sent to different camps. After three or four days stuffed in railroad cars designed for transporting cattle, the prisoners arrived in Westfalenhof in Pomerania (far northeastern Germany) and were marched to Oflag IID near Gross Born to join the nearly 6,000 other French army officers there.

The camp itself was large and divided into four blocks. Each block had about 1,500 prisoners. They were housed forty-eight to a room, four rooms to a barrack. Each room had sixteen triple bunk beds, a table, a few chairs or stools, and a wood-burning stove. The toilets and showers were in separate outbuildings. In the first few months, the prisoners were not permitted to circulate between the blocks and they were assigned rooms. Twice a day, once in the morning and once in late afternoon, they were lined up and counted. The daily rations consisted of thin tea or ersazt coffee for breakfast, a lunch of potatoes with a thin broth, and a supper of soup. Bread was rationed, with one kilo (2.2 lbs.) for five persons.

For several months, Simone had no word on Paul's fate and did not know if he was a prisoner or dead or had escaped to Spain or England. She finally received notice from the Red Cross in early August that he was a prisoner of war and she began a steady correspondence, limited by the Germans to one letter, two postcards, and one package per month. Paul learned from these letters that Simone was pregnant with their third child. Noëlle was born on November 30, 1940. Paul would not see his daughter until she was almost five years old.

After several months, the Germans began repatriating some of the prisoners of war. Veterans of the First World War and those who were injured or sick were the first to be sent back to France. In October, most of the Catholic priests among them were moved to another camp. By Christmas of 1940, the population of the camp had declined by half, to 3,000 officers. From that point on, there were only twenty-one in a room and they were permitted to circulate among the blocks. In fact, they were given the privilege of reassigning rooms and roommates so that they would be more compatible. Those who wanted to spend their time reading would no longer have to tolerate those who wanted to play checkers.

As a result of this possibility of reassigning rooms, Paul found himself in Block II, Barrack 37, Room 4, with other intellectuals and university professors such as Paul-André Lesort, Mikel Dufrenne, and Roger Ikor. They had the right to ask for one book a month from the Swiss Red Cross, so they collated their reading lists and shared books.

The prisoners were permitted to form interest groups and participate in sports, board games, theater, language classes, musical groups, and, later, to organize university courses. The German guards were either veterans of World War I or some of the less capable soldiers. They were in constant fear of being sent to the Russian front,and their principal interest was in not attracting the attention of the Gestapo. This meant that there could be no escapes and no uprisings. Thus, everyone, prisoners and guards, had good reason to find as many pastimes as possible for the prisoners.

Paul spent much of his time reading the complete works of Karl Jaspers, a German existentialist philosopher. In fact, Ricoeur's first major work, *Freedom and Nature: The Voluntary and the Involuntary*, is modeled after Jaspers' *Philosophy of Existence*. Shortly after the war, Paul and Mikel Dufrenne jointly wrote a book on Karl Jaspers. Paul had met Gabriel Marcel in 1934 and was greatly influenced by him. He even received letters from Marcel when he was in the POW camp. Marcel's handwriting was so difficult to read that it took Paul and the German censor hours to decipher it. After the war, they became lifelong friends and Paul always credited Marcel for his influence on Paul's philosophy.

Some prisoners kept careful diaries or journals in which they recorded some of the events and their feelings about them or their imprisonment in general. Thanks to his notes, Roger Ikor wrote an interesting memoir of those five years on the occasion of the thirtieth anniversary of his release. His book, *Pour une fois écoute, mon enfante* ("For once, listen to me, my son") is a chronicle, memoir, and commentary on his captivity, as told to his son.[3] Paul-André Lesort wrote a prizewinning novel,[4] and many others also wrote novels.

3. Roger Ikor, *Pour une fois éoute, mon enfant* (Paris: Editions Albin Michel, 1975). My accounts of the prisoner of war camp and the incidents there and during their captivity are drawn from this book and from taped interviews with Paul-André Lesort.

4. Paul-André Lesort, *Les Reins et les Coeurs* (Paris: Plon, 1946). See also his book *Quelques jours de Mai-Juin 40: Mémoire, Témoignage, Histoire* (Paris: Editions du Seuil, 1992).

Paul read and wrote philosophy. His camp journals are the outlines and first drafts of his first major work, *Freedom and Nature*. They show him working and reworking some of the principal themes of the will, the relation between freedom and constraint, and the concept of "consent." In 1943, he was able to obtain a copy of Husserl's *Ideen I*. Because of a lack of paper, Paul translated it from German into French in the most incredibly minuscule handwriting imaginable in the margins of the book. He was able to do seventy-eight pages of the translation while in the camp. After the war, Paul published the completed translation with his commentary, starting his career as a commentator and critic of Husserl, and launching his worldwide reputation as a leading proponent of phenomenology.[5]

The "university within the camp" began almost immediately, during the summer of 1940. Paul-André Lesort reports that Ricoeur gave a "Lecture on Nietzsche" on July 17.[6] In the beginning, it was principally a pastime, since most of the prisoners thought that the war would end soon and they would be back in France. As the war as well as their imprisonment dragged on, the "university" became better organized, with more regular courses aimed at replicating an academic year. By 1943, they had received permission from the minister of education in Vichy to give examinations, and later, after the was was over, the French government validated some of the university degrees earned in the camp. So, intellectually, those years were not wasted, even though the surroundings were depressing and basic human needs were only minimally met.

The politics of the camp shifted gradually from the majority favoring Marshal Pétain and his post-armistice Vichy government to support for General de Gaulle and his Free French Forces based in England. Among the socialists and pacifists such as Ricoeur, the debate was whether their pacifism in the late 30s actually led to the war. They were torn between their feelings of pacifism and the threatening rise of Nazism in Germany. They had been even more torn between their pacifism and isolationism on the one hand and their democratic and socialist values on the other during the Spanish Civil War between the Republicans and the Nationalists led by Francisco Franco. Paul has claimed, "While we were fighting the pseudo-fascists in France in 1938 and 1939, the real fascists in Germany were rearming and preparing for war."[7]

Escapes from the camp were difficult and rare. Not only would a prisoner have to escape from the camp itself, but he would have to make it by foot or by train all the way across Germany and through occupied France to the southern

---

5. Edmund Husserl, *Idées directrices pour une phénoménologie*, trans. Paul Ricoeur (Paris: Éditions Gallimard, 1950). The German edition, *Ideen zu einer reinen phaenomenologie und phaenomenologischen philosophie*, was originally published in 1913.

6. Taped interview with Paul-André Lesort at his home in Versailles, June 1982.

7. See the interview with Paul Ricoeur, July 8, 1991, below, pp. 127.

part of France, which was not occupied. If he were caught in civilian clothing, he could be shot on sight. All packages were searched and civilian clothes were confiscated. There were frequent searches of the barracks. Letters, sent and received, were carefully censored. On at least two occasions, escapees were shot. In one case, a prisoner had made it past the barbed-wire enclosure and then was shot. In another incident, a group had dug a long tunnel from under their barracks to outside of the enclosure. They planned a night escape. Just as the first of 17 prisoners came up out of the tunnel, a German machine gun opened fire, killing the first man out. The guards had found the exit of the tunnel and had set up an ambush. According to Roger Ikor's estimate, there were 78 escapees, but only 14 or 15 made it back to France.

The principal social unit in the camp was the *popote*, the small group of eight to twelve prisoners who shared a room and ate together. In the early days of their captivity, when there were 6,000 prisoners in the camp, they were divided by the Germans into blocks, barracks, and rooms. The forty-eight per room of the first months gradually became twenty-four as half of the prisoners were repatriated. Once the Germans permitted the prisoners to rearrange themselves according to their interests, the intellectuals sought out other intellectuals to form a *popote*, while those interested in theater, or sports, or politics formed their own *popotes*.

The other social structure in the camp was provided by the military hierarchy, with the senior colonel among the prisoners acting as French commandant. It was he who represented all of the prisoners to the Germans and who handled grievances, special requests, and who, at the same time, was responsible for the conduct of his subordinate officers. The person in this position changed frequently as the senior colonels—all of whom had served in World War I—were repatriated.

The first social problem which had to be solved—as it must be solved in any society—was the rule or principle for the distribution of goods. By late August of 1940, letters and packages began to arrive. The prisoners were permitted to receive one package per month. Their families and friends could send them clothes, blankets, books, and food. The real question was how to fairly share the food in the packages. Prisoners whose families lived in the cities would receive little, if any, food since their families had barely enough for themselves. Those whose families lived in rural areas, especially in the nonoccupied south of France, would receive bountiful packages of coffee, tea, butter, jams, cured meats, and so forth. This created the initial inequality.

The alternatives of the recipient not sharing anything—or being obliged to share everything with everyone—were impractical. The first defied the natural sympathy which is inevitable in such situations; the second was physically impossible: one kilo of sausage divided by six thousand? The unit of distribution was determined to be the *popote*, a group sufficiently small and close. The distribution also presupposed that there would be a steady stream of packages and everyone would contribute to the sum of goods distributed, according to what they received from their families.

The French were not the only prisoners of war at Gross Born. About 500 meters away from the French camp, the Germans built, in August of 1941, a camp for Russian prisoners of war. It was close enough that the borders of the two camps permitted the French to see what was happening in the Russian camp and, on rare occasions, to talk to the Russian prisoners. The practices in the two camps were entirely different: The Germans treated the French prisoners correctly, in strict accordance with the Geneva Accords. Their lives were not pleasant since they were frequently cold and never had enough to eat, but the situation for the Russian prisoners was far worse. Russia had refused to sign the Geneva Accords. For this and the other well-known historical reasons, the Germans visited humiliation, cruelty, and frequently death on the Russian POWs. The French could see the horrible physical condition of the Russian prisoners and could see them daily burying their dead in a trench-grave at the back of their camp. According to Roger Ikor, only 1,400 Russian prisoners remained alive out of the 4,000 who were initially imprisoned there.

In May of 1942, after twenty-three months at Gross Born, the entire group of French prisoners was moved to another camp, Arnswald. The occupants of this camp, Polish prisoners captured in 1939, were moved to Gross Born.

The conditions at Arnswald were far superior to those at Gross Born. Originally, Arnswald was a barracks for German troops. Each building was made of stone blocks, with good windows and adequate lighting and heating. Life within the camp continued much as before. There were more rooms that could be used for classes, study, a library, and other activities. The *Université de l'Oflag* (University of the Prison Camp) became better organized. Paul and his *popote* were assigned to Block III, Room 205.

At the beginning of their imprisonment, the French officers were confident that the war would soon be over and all of them would be repatriated. France was already defeated and they thought the Battle of Britain would begin in early 1941. Instead, the Germans were unable to defeat the Royal Air Force and could not mount an invasion. In the meantime, Hitler ordered an attack on Russia. At first this was seen as a positive move which would help end the war even sooner, but as soon as the German troops became bogged down outside of St. Petersburg in the winter of 1941, the French officers suspected that they would be prisoners indefinitely.

When the Americans declared war on Germany and Japan in December of 1941, there was a feeling of euphoria. This war, just like the First World War, would soon be over. But instead of attacking the Germans in occupied France or Belgium, the American and British carried on the war in North Africa and then Italy. The Americans were also preoccupied with the Japanese in the Pacific. By 1943, the remaining 3,000 prisoners in Oflag IIB at Arnswald began to lose hope of ever being repatriated.

They had managed to construct a clandestine radio out of parts cleverly hidden in sausages and cakes of butter sent from home. Daily they listened to the BBC and quietly circulated the news from barracks to barracks, first by word of mouth, then by hand-copied news reports. The prisoners were encouraged by the German losses on the Russian front and the progress of the Americans in Italy. Doubt turned to hope when they learned of the Allied landings in Normandy in June of 1944. During the fall of 1944, they followed the progress of the Russians as they moved west and that of the Allies who were by then entering Germany. They knew then that the end of their imprisonment was approaching.

During the night of January 28, 1945, the German guards told the French prisoners to gather together their belongings. The next day they would begin a long march to their next camp, 350 kilometers to the southwest. Warsaw had fallen to the Russians in the preceding weeks and Russian troops were about to encircle the camp. At 9:00 A.M. on the 29th, they were assembled in the middle of the camp, given a small amount of bread and sausage, and they began to walk west in the snow. Many of the prisoners had made sleds out of their bed boards and loaded their belongings on them for the journey. At 11:00 P.M. they stopped for the night at Plonzig, some 25 kilometers to the west of Arnswald. Some of the prisoners slept in a church, others in nearby barns, and yet others on the snow outside.

The next day, they walked 21 kilometers to Pyritz, and this time Paul Ricoeur and his *popote* took shelter in a barn. The next day, after a long discussion, they decided to remain there. Their German guards simply told them they would be captured or shot by the SS as escapees, or worse, they would be captured by the advancing Russians. They decided to take their chances with the Russians. They stayed at the farm, sleeping and eating, for four more days. Then, in the middle of the night, a fierce battle was fought between the Germans and the Russians very near the farm. The stone barn was shelled. On February 8 they headed east, both to avoid the pitched battle to the west and in hopes of being liberated by the Russians.

A few kilometers to the east, they took refuge from the shelling at another farm, where they stayed for more than a week. In eleven days, they had gone only 6 kilometers. Soon they fell back into the hands of the Germans, but this time it was different. They were treated to a good meal, then put on a train for another camp just southwest of Stettin. Here they found themselves mingled with prisoners of ten nationalities, Hungarian and German soldiers, and an assortment of civilians. At the end of February, they were put on a train for the west. They spent a few days at an intermediary camp, Sandborstel, before arriving at their final camp, Wietzendorf. Here they were reunited with their fellow prisoners from Arnswald who had walked the 350 kilometers in five weeks. They were haggard, half-starved, and completely exhausted. Those who, with Paul Ricoeur, remained behind on the farms, had eaten well for several weeks and made the journey by train were in far better condition. The trip to Sandborstel was in a passenger train. The short, 24-kilometer trip from there to Oflag 83 at Wietzendorf was made in cattle cars. It took over thirty hours because of the condition of the track.

In mid-April (Lesort's notes say the 22nd) they were finally liberated by the Canadians, but they were not immediately allowed to return to France. First, they were billeted in the nearby town of Bergen, where the inhabitants were forced by the British to evacuate their houses and shops. This was done not only to make room for the freed French prisoners, but as a punishment for the concentration camp of Bergen-Belsen which was just a few kilometers away.

On the fourth of May, they were loaded on British trucks and taken to a railhead. From there, they went by train to Lille where they were once again put in a "camp" for repatriated prisoners. A few days—and much paperwork—later, they were released. Paul Ricoeur arrived in Paris on May 9, 1945—almost five full years after he was captured—and was met at the Gare du Nord by Simone. They spent several days in Paris celebrating and then went to Rennes where Paul saw his five-year old daughter, Noëlle, for the first time, and was reunited with his two sons, Simone's parents, and his aunt Adèle.

Postwar Years

DURING the few days Paul and Simone were in Paris at a *pension,* they met André Philip. Paul was familiar with Philip's political activism which joined thought and action in the service of socialism. André Philip told them about the remarkable town of Le Chambon-sur-Lignon, near Le Puy in the Massif Central of southern France. This mostly Protestant village, under the leadership of Pastor André Trocmé and his wife, Magda, had given refuge to more than 2,500 Jews, both French and foreign, who were trying to escape the Nazi genocide. All during the war, refugees would arrive in the village by train, car, bicycle, or on foot. They would go first to the presbytery where the Trocmés would find them a place to hide in the houses of the village and nearby farms. Fleeing children, mostly Jewish, were given shelter in several boarding houses. They were educated in a

Protestant school, Collège Cévenol. André Philip's wife and family lived in Le Chambon during the Occupation, while he escaped to England and fought with the Free French Forces of General De Gaulle. It was André Philip who suggested that Paul might want to teach at the collège there.

Paul and Simone agreed to try Collège Cévenol during a summer school course in August. They went there and decided to stay for several years. Paul was attracted by its defiant pacifism and its devoted Protestantism. It was also a peaceful place where he could recuperate and regain his physical health and slowly relaunch his academic career. It was a place where he could become re-united and reacquainted with his wife and children. During this period, Paul taught general philosophy and the history of philosophy part-time and also had a research post with the Centre National de la Recherche Scientifique (CNRS). They would remain in Le Chambon until the fall of 1948.

In the summer of 1947, on July 10 to be exact, Paul and Simone's fourth child was born. They named this son Olivier in honor of the peace which followed the five long years of war. During the same summer, Paul met Albert Camus in an unexpected and amusing way. In 1943, Camus had spent a year recuperating from several illnesses in a family house in Le Panelier, a hamlet just outside of Le Chambon. It was here as well that he and his family spent their summer vaca-tions. In August of 1947, the Collège Cévenol was holding summer courses. One evening, a colloquium was devoted to Camus' book *La Peste*,[8] which had just been published earlier that summer. Ricoeur was reviewing the book and com-menting on several of its themes. During the question period which followed, some questions were asked by members of the audience in the form, "What do you think Camus would say about . . . ?" Paul would give a speculative answer. Unbeknownst to Paul, but known to all of the local audience, Camus was in the room, very amused at Paul's answering questions about what Camus would say. Afterwards, he was introduced to Paul, who was at once both embarrassed and amused by the irony of the situation.

In the several years following his liberation, Ricoeur resumed what would be a life-long career as a prolific writer. Some of the articles and all of the books he published between 1947 and 1950 were begun in some fashion or another during his five years of reading, discussing, and teaching philosophy in the Oflag. The first book he published after the war was *Karl Jaspers et la philosophie de l'ex-istence*,[9] coauthored with his friend and fellow prisoner, Mikel Dufrenne. This

8. Albert Camus, *La Peste* (Paris: Gallimard, 1947). In English as *The Plague*, trans. Stuart Gilbert (New York: Alfred Knopf, 1948).

9. Mikel Dufrenne and Paul Ricoeur, *Karl Jaspers et la philosophie de l'existence*, preface by Karl Jaspers (Paris: Éditions du Seuil, 1947).

work is a careful reading of and commentary on Jaspers' major three-volume work, *Philosophy*.[10] Paul was responsible for the second half of the collaborative work, centered on Jaspers' concept of a "situation-limite," such as death, suffering, war, and evil. These were all concepts that would find a place in Ricoeur's own writings. The second part of Paul's contribution dealt with metaphysics and Transcendence. Jaspers' ideas in this part of his work were also very influential on Ricoeur's treatment of Transcendence and the possibilities of "deciphering" or interpreting the symbolic language in which we describe Transcendence. This is one of the few books by Ricoeur that has not been translated into other languages because it is principally a reading of and commentary on Jaspers' work.

A year after the publication of his first book, Paul authored a second book in the same genre of reading and commentary, this time a comparative study, *Gabriel Marcel et Karl Jaspers: Philosophie du mystère et philosophie du paradoxe*.[11] Here, he takes certain themes such as the human condition, human existence, the critique of knowledge, and the existential method and shows how Marcel and Jaspers treats each of them. In the second part of the book, he takes principal categories of each philosopher's work and compares them to one another. For example, he compares Marcel's "incarnation" with Jaspers' "situation-limite," as well as the manner in which each one deals with freedom, communication, and Transcendence. This book, because of its nature as a secondary source, was not translated into other languages.

During his five years as a prisoner, Ricoeur was able to obtain a copy of Edmund Husserl's *Ideen* in German. At the time, it had been translated into English but not French. He was familiar with the English translation from before the war. Paul translated the book himself into French. During his time in Le Chambon, he finished his translation and wrote an elaborate introduction and running commentary on this most difficult and important book. It was published in 1950 and constituted his minor thesis for his *Doctorat d'Etat* (Doctorate of the State)—the highest academic degree obtainable in France.

For his friends of Oflag IIB, Roger Ikor and Paul-André Lesort, the forced leisure was a time of preparing and writing first drafts of novels which would be published just after the war. For Ricoeur, it was a time to write the first draft of his first major work, *Le Volontaire et l'involontaire*. He sketched outlines and wrote sections of it in his journals and on scraps of paper.

In 1948, Paul was called to succeed Jean Hyppolite as *Maitre de conférences* in the history of philosophy at the University of Strasbourg. This began an eight-

---

10. Karl Jaspers, *Philosophie* (Berlin, 1932).

11. Paul Ricoeur, *Gabriel Marcel et Karl Jaspers. Philosophie du mystère et philosophie du paradoxe* (Paris: Temps Présent, 1948).

year period of especially intense philosophical productivity and, as Simone said many years later, "the happiest days of our lives." When they went to Strasbourg, their oldest child, Jean-Paul was eleven and the youngest, Olivier, was just over one year old. When Paul was in Paris in 1934, studying for his *agrégation,* he had met Gabriel Marcel at one of Marcel's famous "Friday afternoons." Marcel would welcome into his home students, colleagues, foreign visitors, and others who wanted to spend several hours with him discussing philosophy, and in particular, whatever problems or philosophical questions Marcel had been reading and writing about during the week. In Strasbourg, the Ricoeurs continued that tradition, only it was Sunday afternoons when Paul and Simone would receive friends, students, colleagues, and anyone who wanted to discuss politics, religion, philosophy, history, or current events. These were pleasant and exciting afternoons for all of the Ricoeurs as the discussions were frequently animated, but always cordial, and sometimes lasted well into the evening.

In 1950, both of Ricoeur's doctoral theses were published. The minor thesis was his translation of and commentary on Husserl's *Ideen I,* while the major thesis was *Le Volontaire et l'involontaire* (translated into English as *Freedom and Nature: The Voluntary and the Involuntary*).[12] This work is the result of the conjunction of several lines of influence from Ricoeur's reading. Husserl's influence is obvious in the "eidetic" method which guides this book, while the very subject, human freedom and constraints on freedom, comes from Ricoeur's reflections on the existential themes in the work of Marcel and Jaspers. He was also strongly influenced by Maurice Merleau-Ponty's book, *The Phenomenology of Perception,* in two distinct ways. He agreed with Merleau-Ponty that Husserl's phenomenological method could be used in the philosophical exploration of a concept, such as perception or freedom, without following Husserl into the idealism of his *Cartesian Meditations* or *Ideas I.* On the other hand, Ricoeur wanted to move beyond Husserl's and Merleau-Ponty's fascination with "representative acts of consciousness" such as knowing, imagining, and perceiving and treat the affective and volitional sphere of consciousness.

The central theme of the first volume of Ricoeur's *Phenomenology of the Will* is human freedom, and the work is, in many ways, an indirect refutation of Jean-Paul Sartre's famous book, *Being and Nothingness.* Ricoeur says in his autobiography[13] that Sartre's work aroused in him "only a distant admiration, but no conviction." Nevertheless, the absolute freedom that Sartre ascribes to man is tempered

---

12. Paul Ricoeur, *Philosophie de la volonté. I. Le volontaire et l'involontaire* (Paris: Aubier, 1950). In English as *Freedom and Nature: The Voluntary and the Involuntary,* trans. E. V. Kohák (Evanston: Northwestern University Press, 1966).

13. Paul Ricoeur, "Intellectual Autobiography," in *Library of Living Philosophers: Paul Ricoeur,* ed. Louis Hahn (Chicago: Open Court, 1995): 11.

in Ricoeur's analysis by the ever-present involuntary which is not an obstacle to freedom as much as it is its negative condition. Ricoeur claims that there is a reciprocity between the voluntary and the involuntary and that they form a dialectic rather than a dichotomy.

The description of the will begins with an account of the "eidetic method" — derived from Husserl. This means, put as simply as possible, that Ricoeur does a conceptual analysis of the will, or modes of willing, and abstracts, for the purposes of this analysis, any consideration of empirical description and any consideration of evil or Transcendence (God). He takes up the question of evil in the second volume of his trilogy, entitled "Finitude and Culpability." He also projected a third volume devoted to Transcendence. This "Poetics of the Will," as he called it, has never been written. He now says that he was caught up in youthful imprudence in announcing such an ambitious plan, but he was fascinated with Jaspers' trilogy of which the third volume was also devoted to Transcendence.

Ricoeur began his description of the concept of willing by asking, what do we mean when we say "I will"? He says we mean "I decide," "I move my body," and "I consent." For each of these modes of willing, a voluntary aspect is necessarily intertwined with a corresponding involuntary aspect. For example, when we decide or make a decision, it is motivated, and our motives have their origin in our bodily condition, such as hunger, thirst, and so forth. Even a person who goes on a hunger strike has weighed his hunger against other values. So, involuntary conditions provide the fundamental "range of motivations," from which, among which, compared to which, we make our decisions. All of our decisions are made in a context of needs, desires, and conditions which are presented to us.

With respect to voluntary action or motion, I move my body in order to do something, say, effect a decision. The primary experience of the involuntary is effort, the resistance of the body. Two aspects of the involuntary corresponding to voluntary movement are emotion and habit. Habit, for example, is a trained or acquired involuntary movement at the service of voluntary movement—or, in some cases, as its impediment. It is in this section of the book that Ricoeur gives his most extensive account of the "lived body" or "personal body" (*corps propre*). Our bodies are objects like other objects in the physical and biological world, but unlike other objects, *we are our bodies*. Following Marcel and Merleau-Ponty, Ricoeur is fighting against traditional dualism which puts consciousness and corporality into two mutually exclusive categories. Even Sartre struggles with traditional dualism and substitutes for it another dualism, that of the "*être-pour-soi*" and "*être-en-soi*," "being-for-itself" and "being-in-itself."

The third mode of willing is consent. Its involuntary correlate is the absolute involuntary, made up of character, the unconscious, and life itself, represented by birth and death. To these, we can only consent or refuse our consent. In Ricoeur's analysis of the will, the voluntary is always reciprocal with the involuntary, but there is an inverse relation between them as we go from decision, where the involuntary is a field of possible motivations; to voluntary movement, where the involuntary is resistance to effort, emotion, and habit; to consent, where the involuntary is almost complete. Notice that the voluntary aspect diminishes in the face of an increasing involuntary.

This book is extremely important because it sets out some themes and methods which remain almost constant in Ricoeur's philosophical work, from beginning to end. For example, virtually all of his work can fit under the rubric of "philosophical anthropology," from the explicit descriptions of the modes of willing, through man's confrontation with evil, to the interpretation of symbolic and poetic language, to deeper understanding of the human condition through Freud's work, to the essential connection between narrative and time, and ending in the study of personal identity. Second, Ricoeur has an abiding interest in the analysis of human action, in all of its forms. Some of his work on action is "eidetic" and abstract, such as *Le volontaire,* while other work is very direct and practical, like his political essays. One of his most important articles offers the methods of understanding texts as a model for understanding human action. He takes as the fundamental feature of narrative Aristotle's idea that a narrative is "a creative imitation of human action."

On April 29, 1950, Paul Ricoeur received his *Doctorat-ès-lettres* and his theses were given a prize from the Society of the Friends of Jean Cavaillès, a special distinction and honor. Jean Cavaillès was an important French philosopher who was killed by the Germans for his resistance activities during the Occupation.

The joy of this springtime of academic success was marred by the sudden death, on March 22, of Ricoeur's friend Emmanuel Mounier. Mounier was a Catholic intellectual who in 1932 started the journal *Esprit,* which was to be the principal organ for the expression of Christian socialist and pacifist ideas before and after the Second World War. Mounier's views, which he called "personalism," are characterized by Christian, especially Catholic, spirituality, a complete opposition to totalitarian, collectivist states and to bourgeois capitalistic states. He advocated an existential concern for the individual, a democratic socialism, and a qualified pacifism. He warned against the injustices of capitalism, the excesses of nationalism, and the dangers of collectivism. The advent of the Second World War forced him to admit that pacificism was limited, since on occasion, such as fighting Nazism, war was morally necessary.

Ricoeur was attracted to all of these views since he was himself a socialist and pacifist. He first met Mounier in Rennes when he was a university student. Mounier was invited to give a talk there on his political views. After the war, Ricoeur attended some conferences at Mounier's home in Chatenay Malabry, a suburb south of Paris. In 1939, Mounier had purchased a large abandoned property in a state of total disrepair. The property was walled, with a large park, a principal residence, a second house, and garages (formerly a carriage house with servants' apartments above). The property was known as *Les murs blancs* (The White Walls) because the high stone and concrete walls were frequently whitewashed. Mounier's dream was to create a commune of individual apartments occupied by members of the *Esprit* team, where they could form an intellectual community. Mounier's project was interrupted by the war, but afterwards, the two large houses were divided into six apartments owned cooperatively by himself and his friends.

Ricoeur paid his respects to his friend and mentor in an article, "Emmanuel Mounier: A Personalist Philosopher," first published in the December 1950 issue of *Esprit*. This article is a long intellectual biography reviewing the development of Mounier's philosophy and paying hommage to its influence on Ricoeur and on a whole generation of French intellectuals.

For the next several years, Ricoeur's academic and personal life in Strasbourg followed a sort of tranquil rhythm. He taught his classes in the history of philosophy. Each year he would read all of the works of a major philosopher and devote one of his classes to that philosopher during the next year. He published numerous articles on various aspects of Husserl's philosophy. Also, he continued working on the second volume of the *Philosophy of the Will*.

In 1953, the Ricoeur's last child, Etienne, was born. The five children now ranged in age from newborn to Jean-Paul's sixteen. Paul's aunt, Adèle, lived with the family in their spacious home. During the summers, they all went to Préfailles, to a house Adèle had purchased in 1934. Préfailles was a small, largely Protestant resort village near Pornic on the south coast of Brittany, very near the estuary of the Loire River. The large garden and the nearness of the beach made it a perfect place for the children. Paul's daily regime was to read in the morning and to take long walks along the coast in the late afternoon. He prepared his classes and wrote many articles there. Their two months at Préfailles were—and still are—very important to the Ricoeurs.

In 1955, Paul made his first trip to the United States. He visited Haverford College, near Philadelphia, at the invitation of the Quakers with whom he was so closely associated at the College Cévenol in Chambon-sur-Lignon. He also visited Montreal on this trip. In the same year, he went to the People's Republic of China as a member of a delegation appointed by the French Ministry of Education at the invitation of the Chinese government. His impressions of China are reported in several articles published in early 1956 in *Esprit* and in other journals.[14]

The Sorbonne

IN THE SPRING of 1956, Ricoeur received the crowning achievement of any provincial professor: He was called to the Sorbonne in Paris, succeeding Raymond Bayer in the Chair of General Philosophy. Shortly thereafter, he was given a second honor, an invitation to live at Les Murs Blancs. At the time, all but one of the apartments were occupied by Mounier's friends and his widow. All of them shared Mounier's philosophical views and certainly his dream of as an intellectual commune of independent families, each living in their own apartment but as co-owners of the common park and orchard.

The principal building at Les Murs Blancs is a neoclassical three-story rectangular house built in 1836. A second house was constructed in 1899 in the gabled, multicolored native stone and gray-cut stone style popular in France at the turn of the century. This building had a large orangerie or greenhouse on the first floor, with-floor-to ceiling windows. The Ricoeurs were invited to turn the orangerie into their apartment. The Mouniers—and Mrs. Mounier until her death in 1990—lived on the third floor of the principal residence. The first floor was occupied by the Domenachs. Jean-Marie Domenach was a regular contributor to *Esprit* and later the editor of the journal for many years. The second floor was the apartment of Paul Fraisse, a professor of psychology at the Sorbonne, who was a partner with Mounier from the very beginning and to this day is still the manager of the common property.

The secondary residence was originally built for the children and grandchildren of the owners of the principal house. The whole main floor was designed to be a greenhouse and winter garden. Jean Baboulène occupied the third floor while the well-known historian Henri Marrou lived on the second floor. During the time it took to convert the greenhouse into an apartment, Paul commuted from Strasbourg to Paris. In 1957, the whole family moved into their new residence in Chatenay-Malabry (birthplace of Voltaire).

During the late 50s and early 60s, Paul's classes on Kant, Nietzsche, Aristotle, Husserl and phenomenology, and symbolic language were extremely popular. Often, more than a thousand students tried to crowd into one of the amphithe-

14. See, for example, Paul Ricoeur, "Certitudes et incertitudes d'úne révolution," *Esprit* (La Chine, porte ouverte) 24 (1956), no. 1, January, 5–28. "Note critique sur 'Chine ouverte,'" *Esprit* 22 (1956), no.6, June, 897–910. "Questions sur la Chine," *Christianisme sociale* 64 (1956), no. 5–6, May-June, 319–35.

atres at the Sorbonne to hear his lectures. He began receiving invitations to read papers at other universities in France and in Europe.

In 1955, Ricoeur published *History and Truth*[15], a collection of his articles which had appeared in *Esprit* and elsewhere. These articles were on a wide range of topics, including the history of philosophy and the philosophy of history, on the relation between God and man, on personalism, on the question of political power. The collection ends with a dense and difficult discussion of the role of negation in philosophy. This article is a veiled critique of Sartre and a precurser of Ricoeur's own *Fallible Man*.

Another very significant article that Ricoeur published in 1955 is "La parole est mon royaume,"[16] a declaration of his own view of the importance and role of teaching and a thorough critique of the overemphasis on "work" of the Marxists and other critics of the university. It is remarkable that this is one of the very few of his articles which has not been translated into English. It begins,

> What do I do when I teach? I talk. I have no other way of making a living and I have no other dignity; I have no other way of transforming the world and no other influence on other people. Speaking is my work; language is my kingdom. My students, for the most part, will have another relation with things and with people; they will construct something with their hands; or perhaps they will speak and write in businesses, in stores, in administrative offices, but their language will not be the language which teaches. It will be part of an action, an order, a plan, or the beginning of an action. My speaking does not begin any action, it does not command any action which can be involved, directly or indirectly, in any production. I speak only to communicate to the younger generation the knowledge and the research of the older generation. This communication by speech of acquired knowledge and research in progress is my reason for being, my profession, and my honor. I am not jealous of those who are "in the real world" who have a "grip on reality," as are certain teachers who are unhappy with themselves. My reality and my life is the kingdom of words, of sentences, and of discourse itself.

The rest of the article addresses questions peculiar to the French university system in the 1950s, such as the continued importance of Latin and classical literature, the system of examinations, including the *agrégation*, and the role of the humanities in the education of all students. What is important is that this article

15. Paul Ricoeur, *Histoire et vérité* (Paris: Éditions du Seuil, 1955). A second edition was published in 1964 and a third in 1967. The subsequent editions contained additional articles. The third edition was reprinted in 1978.

16. Paul Ricoeur, "La parole est mon royaume," *Esprit* (Réforme de l'enseignement) 23 (1955), no. 2, February, 192–205 (My translation).

is the beginning of a long and rigorous critique of the French university system that Ricoeur wrote over a thirteen-year period, culminating in his becoming *Doyen* at the University of Paris-Nanterre.

During this decade, Ricoeur worked tirelessly on the second volume of his *Philosophy of the Will*. In 1960, he published *Finitude and Culpability* in two parts, *Fallible Man* and *The Symbolism of Evil*.[17] The first book, *Fallible Man*, is a transcendental study of the conditions under which evil or sin is possible. The method is Kantian, and the theme is existential. Ricoeur wants to remove the "brackets" from evil or sin and go beyond his "eidetic" analysis of the "pure will" found in *The Voluntary and the Involuntary*. After having described the will as such, he wants to extend his analysis to a will which chooses evil. He asks, under what conditions is evil possible and how can a will which is essentially free bind itself in the commission of sin? His answer is very Cartesian in the sense that he finds a disproportion—to use Pascal's expression—not between the will and understanding, as Descartes claimed in his explanation of how error is possible, but within the will itself. Human freedom is always and at once infinitely open and limited. This "disproportion" within us between our possibilities and our limitations renders us "fragile." Our soul is condemned to be restless. We are capable of owning things, of exercising our powers, and of being loved and respected. But when will we ever have enough? When will our power be secure? When will other people respect and esteem us enough? This "restlessness" or "disproportion" is not evil or sin in itself, but it opens us up and leaves us vulnerable to temptation and sin.

In the second part of the "empirics" of the will, *The Symbolism of Evil*, Ricoeur moves from the structural possibility of evil in our very human nature to the actual expression of evil and our sinfulness in the symbols in which we express evil: stain, burden, errancy, separation, or captivity. This book represents Ricoeur's first venture into a philosophical analysis of symbolic language, an interest which became a permanent feature of his philosophy. His principal thesis is that evil is always spoken of metaphorically or symbolically. There is no direct or literal language of sinfulness. Therefore, we must approach our actual avowal of sin through the interpretation of symbols or double-meaning expressions. His second thesis is that the myths of the origin of the world, such as the "battle of the Titans," or "the Orphic myth of the good soul trapped in an evil body," or, to be sure, "the Adamic myth of temptation in the Garden of Eden," are first-

---

17. Paul Ricoeur, *Finitude et Culpabilité I: L'homme faillible* (Paris: Aubier, 1960). *Finitude et Culpabilité II: La Symbolique du mal* (Paris: Aubier, 1960). In English as *Fallible Man*, trans. Charles Kelbley (Chicago: Henry Regnery, 1965), and *The Symbolism of Evil*, trans. Emerson Buchanan (New York: Harper and Row, 1967).

order explanations offered throughout history of the origin of evil in the world. He concludes this book with an essay on how symbols can provide a fertile field for philosophical analysis.

This thesis is completely contrary to the claim that philosophy must avoid symbolic language or that the goal of philosophy is to convert all symbolic language into clear, literal discourse. The most important feature of Ricoeur's philosophy for the twenty years following the publication of *Finitude and Culpability* is the "hermeneutic" turn his phenomenology takes. From this point on, the interpretation of texts and hermeneutic theory move from being a method among other methods to the very center of his philosophical interests.

From the time that Ricoeur came to Paris in 1956, the French political scene was dominated by the civil war in Algeria. This extremely bitter war, begun in 1954, led to the fall of a series of governments under the Fourth Republic, which was a parliamentary form of government. In May of 1958, the government of Premier Pflimlin resigned and President Coty asked the Parliament to invest General De Gaulle with complete power as head of the government. On June 1, the Parliament voted to give him "full powers." As early as 1957, Ricoeur became active in opposition to the French policy of refusing independence to the Arab majority in Algeria and in pursuing a full military war against the Algerian nationalists. He wrote letters and articles in the popular press against the government policy and was very visible in many demonstrations against the war. He was especially incensed about the French practice of using torture to extract information from captured Algerian nationalists (FLN).

At one particularly large gathering at the Mutualité (a large meeting hall on the Left Bank), Ricoeur said, "We do not want to be like those German university professors during the Nazi period who remained silent because they were government employees and because they did not think it was their job to take outside of the university the principles they honored within the university."[18]

In the late spring (end of May, beginning of June) of 1961, three inspectors and several uniformed police knocked on the Ricoeurs' door at 6:00 A.M. They had a search warrant and began a thorough search of the whole house and grounds. Ricoeur had been anonymously accused of hiding arms for the FLN. The police found nothing. However, they also had an arrest warrant and took Paul to the Commissariat of Police in Sceaux, a neighboring suburb of Paris. His passport was confiscated and no one was permitted to speak with him.

Simone was extremely worried and called their friends to alert them to what

18. Michel Winock, *La République se meurt: Chronique 1956–58* (Paris: Éditions du Seuil, 1978): 166.

had happened to Paul. She called a former student of Ricoeur's who at the time had a job as a secretary in President De Gaulle's office. She asked him to intercede directly with De Gaulle. The former student was successful and Paul was released at 8:00 P.M., just before the other detainees were loaded on a train and taken to a detention camp near Lyon, where they were held for a week or two and then released. After his release from the police station in Sceaux, Paul was put under house arrest. The Parisian newspaper, *Le Monde*,[19] published his letter protesting his house arrest and the search of his property. Several weeks later, the house arrest was lifted.

As the war dragged on, both sides in France became extremely polarized and the violence in Algeria was transposed to France itself, especially Paris and Marseilles. The ultraright secret group, the OAS, was especially active in bombing police stations and public places, and in ambushing police and political figures. The Ricoeurs—as well as their neighbors—were publicly identified among the most outspoken of the antiwar protesters. As a consequence, they were afraid that their residence, Les Murs Blancs, would be bombed. Every time a car came down Rue des Grandes Vignes or up Rue Vincent Fayo late at night, they were terrified that a "plastique" (bomb) would come over the wall or that OAS agents would machine-gun the houses.

For several weeks, they got little sleep at night and had to be extremely cautious during the day. Their students volunteered to keep watch at night from the rooms over the carriage house, which gave a good view of the intersection. Each family took turns in providing food to the students. This was the only way they could relax. After several months, the armistice was negotiated and the danger passed. The OAS continued its urban guerilla activities for more than a year after the truce was signed in the summer of 1962. Their attacks included an ambush of General De Gaulle's car at Petit Clamart, only a couple of kilometers from Chatenay Malabry where Ricoeur lives.

In 1960, Paul Ricoeur was one of the most famous and well-known professors in France: His classes at the Sorbonne were jammed and loudspeakers had to be set up in the courtyard so the overflow crowd could hear him. Hundreds of students asked him to direct their theses. His books *Fallible Man* and *The Symbolism of Evil* were widely read and commented on. He wrote many articles on political questions for popular and semipopular journals and magazines, such as *Esprit*. Finally, he was well known as a man of courage and moral integrity for his visible participation in demonstrations against the war in Algeria.

At the same time, the psychiatrist Jacques Lacan was known only in psychoanalytical circles and had not yet achieved the fame he subsequently had. During

19. See *Le Monde*, 18 (1961), no. 5102, June 14, p. 2.

this period, Lacan was looking for a philosophical underpinning for his own theoretical analyses of Freud's works on psychoanalysis. He had hoped that Maurice Merleau-Ponty would become his philosophical "partner," but Merleau-Ponty rejected Lacan's theoretical positions. In 1960, Ricoeur and Lacan presented papers at the same conference at Bonneval and Lacan was very complimentary about Ricoeur's paper, "L'Inconscient" ("The Unconscious").[20] He offered Ricoeur a ride back to Paris in his car and invited him to attend his seminar, hoping that Ricoeur would become his ally.

Ricoeur had been exposed to Freud in the 1930s by his professor, Roland Dalbiez, the first philosopher to write a book on Freud in France. In his first major work, *The Voluntary and the Involuntary*, Ricoeur devoted a considerable part of a chapter to a discussion of the unconscious. But what really brought Ricoeur back to Freud was his work on symbolic language in *The Symbolism of Evil*. From 1958 to 1961, Ricoeur read the entire corpus of Freud's work. In addition, he did attend Lacan's seminars from 1960 until 1963. He gave the Terry Lectures at Yale University in 1961 and a series of eight lectures at Louvain in 1962. These two sets of lectures formed the core of his book on Freud published in 1965, *Freud and Philosophy*.[21]

On the eve of a 1963 colloquium in Rome, Lacan called Ricoeur and asked him what he thought of his theories on Freud. Ricoeur responded that he could not understand them and that he found Lacan to be incoherent and unintelligible. Lacan was furious. In Rome he refused to give his paper and was very contentious in the discussion of Ricoeur's paper. Then, he invited the Ricoeurs to dinner, but abruptly told Ricoeur to pay the bill. After dinner, they were taking a taxi back to the hotel when, partway there, Lacan suddenly got out of the cab and Paul once again had to pay the bill. The next day Lacan apologized to Simone for his rude behavior.[22]

Ricoeur's break with Lacan became extremely hostile after the publication in 1965 of his book on Freud. Lacan had expected to be a central figure in Ricoeur's book and to have his theories prominently featured. Instead, he is barely men-

20. Paul Ricoeur, "Le conscient et l'inconscient," *VIe Colloque de Bonneval: L'inconscient* (Paris: Desclée de Brouwer, 1966). Reprinted in Paul Ricoeur, *Le conflit des interprétations. Essais d'herméneutique* (Paris: Éditions du Seuil, 1969). In English as "Consciousness and the Unconscious," trans. Willis Domingo, in Paul Ricoeur, *The Conflict of Interpretations: Essays in Hermeneutics* (Evanston: Northwestern University Press, 1974).

21. Paul Ricoeur, *De l'interprétation. Essai sur Freud* (Paris: Éditions du Seuil, 1965). In English as *Freud and Philosophy: An Essay on Interpretation*, trans. Dennis Savage (New Haven: Yale University Press, 1970).

22. Elisabeth Roudinesco, *La bataille de cent ans. Histoire de la psychanalyse en France. 2, 1925–1985* (Paris: Éditions du Seuil, 1986). In English as *Jacques Lacan & Co. A History of Psychoanalysis in France, 1925–1985*, trans. Jeffrey Mehlman (Chicago: University of Chicago Press, 1990): 394.

tioned and the only real discussion of an aspect of his theories is relegated to a footnote. Lacan unleashed his disciples, who produced a torrent of criticism of Ricoeur's views. Ricoeur was used to having his philosophical positions attacked, but he was not prepared for the personal and vitriolic criticism he received. His battle with Lacan and the Lacanians even occurred on a familial level. One of the reasons he began attending Lacan's seminar was that his oldest son, Jean-Paul, was a physician training to become a psychiatrist. Jean-Paul, like many psychologists and psychiatrists in France at the time, was attracted to the seemingly radical theories of Lacan. Among other things, Lacan embraced structuralism and repudiated phenomenology. So the battle between the theoreticians became an intergenerational battle between father and son.

Freud and Philosophy is divided into three parts, a "problematic," an "analytic," and a "dialectic." The first part locates psychoanalysis in the philosophical debates on language in general, and symbolic language in particular. Ricoeur calls psychoanalysis a "semantics of desire," or "How do desires achieve speech? How do desires make speech fail, and why do they themselves fail to speak?"[23] Ricoeur's hermeneutics expanded from symbols as double-meaning expressions to the rules for the interpretation of a text whose meaning may be unintelligible on the surface, or texts with multiple meanings.

Ricoeur places Freud among the "masters of suspicion," such as Marx and Nietzsche. All three called into question the naive belief that consciousness is translucent and available to introspection. "What all three attempted, in different ways, was to make their 'conscious' methods of deciphering coincide with the 'unconscious' *work* of ciphering which they attributed to the will to power, to social being, to the unconscious psychism."[24] Freud is to be read as demasking our illusions, and as giving us the rules for the interpretation of the unconscious, as manifested in neurotic symptoms, dreams, and the general unhappiness of modern culture.

But Ricoeur will also end his study of Freud by establishing a dialectic between suspicion and faith, which he says is the opposite of suspicion. The opposite dialectical pole to demasking illusion is the revelation of the sacred. If, to use Merleau-Ponty's term, psychoanalysis is the "archeology of the subject," then there must be a "teleology of the subject." In short, Ricoeur creates a dialectic between psychoanalysis as the interpretation of the unconscious, especially desire, and the eschatalogical hope of all religions to move beyond what we were and what we are to what we can become. In this sense, it was the concept of culpability or guilt which led Ricoeur to his interest in psychoanalysis in the first

23. *Freud and Philosophy: An Essay on Interpretation*, 6.
24. Ibid., 34.

place, and his work on Freud is a continuation of his work on human fragility and the symbolic expressions of sinfulness found in his *Culpability and Finitude*.

The "analytic" portion of the book is a reading of Freud. Ricoeur claims that Freud can be read like any other philosopher and that it is just as possible to give an objective account of his writings as it is in the case of Aristotle or Descartes. Some psychoanalysts, especially Lacanians, disputed this and claimed that Freud's psychoanalysis refers to "an experience which requires apprenticeship and competence, which is a craft and even a technique."[25] Therefore, since Ricoeur is neither an analyst nor has he been psychoanalyzed, he is in no position to write on Freud. Ricoeur responds that Freud did not write for his colleagues and students only, but addressed a general audience. Furthermore, the object of his studies was not human desire and its unconscious manifestations, but "desire in a more or less conflicting relationship with a world of culture, a father and mother, authorities, imperatives, prohibitions, works of art, social ends, and idols."[26] Thus, the very object of psychoanalysis is "the totality of human experience which philosophy undertakes to reflect upon and understand."[27]

In his reading of Freud, Ricoeur moves from Freud's "energetics" as represented in his earliest writings to a "hermeneutics" as developed in his *Interpretation of Dreams*. He continues through a long account of Freud's interpretation of culture and the continual conflict between the individual and his social milieu. Ricoeur's claim, his "bet," is that a relatively neutral reading of Freud is possible, a reading which leaves open a number of possible philosophical interpretations. Much later, in his "Autobiography," Ricoeur admits that there is much more interpretation in any "reading" of a text than he thought at the time.[28]

In his "Dialectic," or philosophical interpretation of Freud, Ricoeur begins with a long and technical discussion of the epistemology of psychoanalysis from which he concludes that psychoanalysis is not an observational science and cannot meet the explanatory norms of the natural sciences. In addition, it is not a kind of phenomenology, even when psychoanalysis is reformulated totally in terms of language and meaning. In fact, the fundamental presupposition of phenomenology, that we have a direct and veridical access to consciousness, is contradicted by the fundamental claims of Freudian psychoanalysis. Ricoeur's conclusion is that psychoanalysis is a hermeneutical science whose object is the "semantics of desire," the intersection of desire and speech, of unconscious struc-

---

25. Paul Ricoeur, "A Philosophical Interpretation of Freud," in *The Conflict of Interpretations*, 163.

26. Ibid., 163.

27. Ibid., 164.

28. See Paul Ricoeur, "Intellectual Autobiography."

tures and the cultural world. Or, the "language of desire is a discourse combining meaning and force."[29]

The main claim in his philosophical interpretation of Freud is that the archeology of the subject in psychoanalysis is dialectically related to a teleology. The point of intersection is the "symbol." The symbolism in dreams is a cultural symbolism. Ricoeur returns to a theme of *Fallible Man* to illustrate how desire, in its origins and its ends, combines an archeology with a teleology. He is referring to the human passions or desires for having, power, and valuation. When will I ever have enough? When will my power be secure? When will I be recognized and valued by other people? Ricoeur says, "It is here that the profound identity of the two hermeneutics, regressive and progressive, may be shown most clearly and forcefully. It is here that the archeology itself, and the telos of the human adventure will be foreshadowed in the endless exegesis of the myths and hidden secrets of our childhood and birth."[30] Ricoeur finishes with an account of Freud's psychoanalysis of religion and confronts it with the hermeneutics of Eliade, Van der Leuuw, Barth, and Bultmann. In the end, there is a conflict of interpretations. Ricoeur says, "it is impossible to construct a psychoanalysis of belief apart from an interpretation and understanding of the cultural productions in which the object of belief announces itself."[31] Both guilt and consolation are central concepts in psychoanalysis and religion. And, according to Ricoeur, the archeological interpretation of Freud calls for, requires even, a teleological interpretation which includes forgiveness and hope.

When Ricoeur's book on Freud was published in the spring of 1965, it achieved great success and attracted extraordinary criticism. Freud was one of the dominant influences on the French intellectual scene, just as Heidegger and Husserl had been a decade earlier. Even though Sartre, Merleau-Ponty, and Ricoeur had all written on Freud much earlier, and Jacques Lacan had been developing his theories since the early 1950s, Freud was really "discovered" by French philosophers, psychoanalysts, and writers in the 1960s. Ricoeur's book was the first that combined a detailed reading along with a philosophical interpretation of Freud and brought together psychoanalysis and philosophy. Nevertheless, Ricoeur was best known as a phenomenologist, and his own version of hermeneutics was not well developed at the time. Phenomenology was very out of fashion in France in the mid–1960s and a strong reaction to it had formed. Lacan and his theories were well known, but, at the time, he had not published a significant book detailing his theoretical constructions.

29. *Freud and Philosophy: An Essay on Interpretation*, 424.
30. Ibid., 515.
31. Ibid., 544.

Lacan was furious with Ricoeur's book. First of all, it usurped his ground: Lacan thought that he and he alone was the authentic French interpreter of Freud. Second, "he had expected to be glorified and found himself misunderstood by a celebrated philosopher who had attended his seminar."[32] Complaining to his entourage that Ricoeur had plagiarized his ideas, Lacan turned his supporters loose to write scathing attacks on Ricoeur and his book.

One particularly vitriolic attack came from J-P Valabréga, who claimed that Ricoeur had taken Lacan's ideas without attribution. Valabrega asks, "Can anyone imagine, to take the most flagrant example, a work of this length which, from the beginning, situates the *theory of language* at the center of his argument without clearly underlining that it is J. Lacan who introduced or reintroduced the study of language into contemporary Freudian research? Nevertheless, that is the case with Mr. Ricoeur."[33] Later in the article, he says, "In proceeding thus, Mr. Ricoeur makes his own many ideas which did not originally belong to him. He gives the impression that all of the theses he develops in his reading of Freud are the fruit of his solitary reflection, which would be an immense and admirable feat, but it is not true."[34]

Paul Ricoeur has written an enormous number of papers and books over his long philosophical career. He had never before written a reply to a critic. He says that it is the job of the critic to criticize and that he has a right to express his disagreement with the author. But in this case, Valabréga stepped over the line. In a scathing reply in the next issue of the same journal, Ricoeur responds to each of Valabréga's accusations. He reminds his critic that he came to Freud by his studies of the symbolism of evil, that he had been giving courses on Freud beginning in 1960, before he was familiar with Lacan's work and before he had attended Lacan's seminars. In general, he says that we appropriate the ideas of all of the philosophers whom we have read—Aristotle, Kant, Descartes, Hegel. But this is true of everyone who enters the intellectual scene. Furthermore, he gives in detail the places in his book where he discusses Lacan's theories and his agreement or disagreement with his theses. He finishes by saying, "Did not Freud also say important things about having and devouring, about money and excrement? Are 'ideas' distinct things which can be owned and stolen? As if the important thing is not the thought that the ideas begin and which no one can say he 'owns'."[35]

In her impressive and exhaustive history of psychoanalysis in France, *Jacques Lacan & Co.*, Elisabeth Roudinesco claims that Ricoeur could not have "stolen"

32. Elisabeth Roudinesco, *Jacques Lacan & Co.*, 395.
33. J.-P. Valabréga, "Comment survivre à Freud," *Critique* 22, January (1966): 75.
34. Ibid., 76.
35. Paul Ricoeur, "Une Lettre de Paul Ricoeur," *Critique* 22, February (1966): 186.

Lacan's ideas because he did not understand them. She says it is remarkable that Ricoeur could have attended Lacan's seminars and read some of his articles and yet there is no evidence that he was influenced by them. Where Ricoeur does speak of Lacan's theories, Roudinesco claims, he has systematically misread or misunderstood them. For Paul, there was no mystery: He wanted to read Freud, not Lacan's version of Freud. Second, he gave a very different interpretation of Freudian concepts, such as the unconscious, or instinct or drive, than did Lacan. Finally, Ricoeur had a larger "architectonic" into which he wanted to fit Freud's writings, and that was the dialectic between suspicion and faith, between symbolic language as illusion and symbolic language as revelation of the sacred. So, there are at least three plausible interpretations to this episode: stolen ideas, total misunderstanding, or the irrelevance of certain theoretical ideas for an overall project.

What this sorry episode does illustrate is the vitriolic and possessive level of intellectual discourse during this period in France, especially among the Lacanians, who were continuously forming and dissolving groups and grouplets, each claiming—or disclaiming—Lacan as the master. But this was a time when political ideas were also debated through demonstrations, and civility was absent from the discussion.

Nanterre

DURING the course of his career as a university professor, Ricoeur had written many articles criticizing certain features of the French university system. In 1964, he wrote an especially influential article for a special issue of *Esprit* dedicated to an in-depth study of the university in France. In this article, "To Make the University" (*Faire l'Université*),[36] Ricoeur lists some of the most critical problems facing the French universities, such as how to deal with the explosion in the number of students. By the end of the 1960s, the Sorbonne had, theoretically, 120,000 students although it was built to accommodate at most 20,000. The curriculum needed to be changed to add professional studies and career preparation to the traditional liberal studies, heavily weighted towards the classics and letters. There was a national uniformity among all universities with respect to curricula, examinations, subjects taught for particular certificates or diplomas. Ricoeur advocated differentiating among universities with respect to curricula and types of subjects taught so that the students would have a wide variety of choices. Students had no opportunities to have contact with their professors and with other students. Professors had no offices in the Sorbonne and had to meet students, on the rare occasions that they did, in nearby cafés. Except for those living in the

---

36. Paul Ricoeur, "Faire l'Université," *Esprit* (Faire l'université) 32, May-June (1964): 1162–72.

Cité Universitaire, students did not live in university residence halls but were scattered all over the city. There was no sense of a campus, no organized student sports or activities, and rarely were any classes small enough for student interaction. Finally, the administration was too centralized in the Ministry of Education and it was too bureaucratic and rigid, exacting a dulling uniformity from all of the French universities.

Ricoeur also complained of the practice of professors at provincial universities living in Paris and commuting once or twice a week to their schools. In addition, since professors were civil servants, it was practically impossible to have visiting foreign professors teach on a short-term basis. He was also critical of the fact that the research function was completely removed from the university and located in another government bureaucracy, the Centre National de Recherche Scientifique (CNRS). Many professors held dual appointments in a faculty and in the CNRS, but their research was conducted in a center apart from the university. Ricoeur ended this scathing critique with these prophetic words: "If this country does not control, by rational choices, the growth of its universities, it will experience the academic explosion as a national cataclysm."[37]

In the spring of 1967, Ricoeur, along with two other colleagues, made the daring and surprising choice to leave the prestige of the Sorbonne for a new campus of the University of Paris being built in the western suburb of Nanterre. His motivation was simple: This new university would permit him and the other professors to build the kind of university he envisioned, one which would avoid the problems he enumerated in his 1964 article. This would be the chance to escape the rigidity—the fossilizing influence—of the Sorbonne, with its centuries of traditions and rules and practices.

A new university at Nanterre, as well as other new campuses, was the response to the enormous overcrowding at the Sorbonne. France, like other countries, had a postwar baby boom which was just reaching college age in the early 1960s. In order to save money, and have a new campus in the western suburbs of Paris, the Ministry of Education bought a former French Air Force maintenance depot at a place whose original name was Nanterre-La Folie. The last part of the name comes from a seventeenth-century expression for a wooded grove, but it was to have other significations as well.

When the first buildings went up, the campus still had its military-base wall, topped with barbed wire, around it. Outside the walls was a "bidonville," or shanty town of hastily constructed shacks, dirt roads, and no running water, sew-

37. Paul Ricoeur, "Faire l'Université," reprinted in *Lectures I: Autour du politique* (Paris: Éditions du Seuil, 1989): 379.

age system, or electricity. This "workers camp" was home to thousands of immigrant workers from North Africa. To make the place even more dismal, there was mud everywhere because of all of the construction. Also, at that time, the only public transportation between Paris and Nanterre was a suburban train from Gare St. Lazare.

From another perspective, Nanterre would be one of the most interesting of French educational experiments because the new university was designed as a campus, with residence halls, a cafeteria, library, swimming pool, sports fields, and a tree-lined quadrangle in the middle. Students would live there and form a community. Nanterre would be an attempt to create the atmosphere of the best American and British residential universities.

Paul Ricoeur, along with his two colleagues from the Sorbonne, Pierre Grappin and Jean Beaujeu, began teaching there in the fall of 1967. In the spring of 1968 the campus experienced some political demonstrations, and a great deal of hostility among students, because the new university was composed of two "faculties" (what Americans would call "colleges"): Law and Letters. The law students were generally from more affluent families and tended to be on the political right. In the Faculty of Letters, on the other hand, students tended to be left or far left. Here, the sociology, philosophy, and history students had visions of remaking a decadent bourgeois society into a workers' paradise, according to the writings of Marx, Mao, and Ché Guevara.

One of the first acts of "official" confrontation came after a meeting of one of the leftist groups, when a student said "Everyone to the girls dormitory!" Unofficial visitation had been taking place since the opening of the dorm, but this was to be a confrontation with the university authorities in order to force them to change the rule against males in the girls dorm. In reality, this was to be the opening shot at all of the authoritarian rules of the "bourgeois state."

The next confrontation took place less than a month later. The new swimming pool was being dedicated by Misoffe, the minister of youth, who had written a well-known book on young people. After his dedicatory speech, a foreign student, Daniel Cohn-Bendit from Germany, engaged the minister in a rapid and hostile exchange of words. Then, Cohn-Bendit proclaimed the ceremony to be over, and the students forced the end of the proceedings by their totally disruptive behavior.

Two weeks later, a band of leftist students occupied the meeting room of the Council of Professors on the top floor of the administration building. This was done to protest the arrest in Paris of two leftist students accused of participating in a bombing attack on the American Express building near the Opéra. The students left the council room the next morning, but less than one week later they invaded the office of the doyen[38] of the Faculty of Letters. Several days later, they forbade certain professors, in particular, René Rémond, a Catholic historian, to teach their classes. The administration was powerless to do anything. The university does not have its own police, and the municipal police can enter the campus, according to French law, only if called by the doyen. Had the university officials called the police, the leftists would have won, since thousands of leftists from all over Paris would have flocked to the campus and a full-scale demonstration would have resulted.

Fortunately for Nanterre, the attention of the leftists and the press was turned to the Sorbonne, where, the day after classes were suspended at Nanterre, hundreds of students in helmets and armed with clubs and chains occupied the courtyard of the Sorbonne. The police were called to clear them out, and a major battle ensued. Three days later, there was another battle between the police and the students in the Latin Quarter. Before the smoke had cleared, 600 students and 345 police had been injured, some severely. This was the beginning of the famous "Events of 1968," which ultimately brought the French economy and government to a standstill and fatally wounded the public prestige of the De Gaulle presidency.

Almost one year later, Paul Ricoeur was elected by the University Council to succeed Jean Beaujeu as doyen of the Faculty of Letters. He chose René Rémond as his "Assesseur," or second-in-command. The situation at Nanterre was this: The events of 1968 slowly died out over the summer and by the fall of 1968 things were more or less back to normal. The most significant piece of legislation to come out of the civil turmoil was the "Loi d'orientation," or a law to reorganize the structure of the French university system. The main elements, which would establish more autonomous universities, administered by presidents elected by university councils, with independent budgets, were still several years away.

During the 1969–70 academic year, Nanterre suffered two problems which were unique to it. First, the remnants of the leftist groups gravitated to Nanterre. This, the newest of the French universities, was perceived to be the weakest link in the weakest institution of the government. To topple the government, the leftists' strategy was to attack at the weakest point. A second grave threat to the campus came from the nearby "bidonvilles." The children of the immigrant workers discovered that the campus was an asylum from the police and they could commit any petty crime there without fear of being caught. These young

---

38. "Doyen," or Dean, was the chief administrative officer of a "Faculty" and was elected by the professors, who also elected a Council of Administration to advise the Doyen. The principal difficulty with this arrangement, as it was then in France, was that the Doyen had no budgetary or personnel authority. These were vested in the Ministry of Education.

men invaded the campus and committed theft, vandalism, muggings, and even sexual assaults.

In mid-January of 1969, the problems started all over again, this time in the Faculty of Law. Students of varying political persuasions tried to prevent their opponents from entering the campus or the law building. They were armed with iron bars and chains. The doyen of the Faculty of Law responded by suspending classes and closing the faculty for several days. This simply meant that the battle would be transferred to the Faculty of Letters. Among other provocations, a small band of leftists prohibited the faculty and administrators from using the cafeteria. Ricoeur and his council, believing that they could not let students dictate where on campus professors went, decided to challenge them. Ricoeur, Rémond, and a few other professors went to the cafeteria for a cup of coffee. Just as Ricoeur approached, a student took a lid from a trash can and acted as though he was going to hit him with it; instead he placed it on Ricoeur's head. Ricoeur was mortified.

Here, a man of peace, a pacifist, a man of reason and argument, a devout believer in mercy and forgiveness, a man gentle in every way, was the target of a physical attack. There were two effects of this incident: The public was outraged and Ricoeur received great sympathy, even from his philosophical and political opponents. Second, on his doctor's orders, Ricoeur took a two-week leave for health reasons.

During his medical leave, the Faculty of Law reopened, with a dozen "appariteurs"—or security guards—present. Almost immediately, a band of leftists grabbed two of them, took their papers away from them, covered them with black paint, and marched them to the Faculty of Letters for a "trial." This incident might have turned into a lynching had a dozen professors and administrators not interposed themselves—at a risk to their own safety—and forced the students to release them. The real irony of the situation became apparent when one of the guards said to a student, "I am a working man from a poor family, and you are the rich son of a wealthy family who is not working; so why are you attacking me in the name of the working class and calling me bourgeois? You are a spoiled bourgeois brat."

Battles between Maoists and Communists continued throughout the month of February. The Communists held a demonstration at the Faculty of Law, drawing Communists from other universities and from the labor unions. The Maoists responded to this demonstration by claiming that the Faculty of Law belonged to them and they would not permit the Communists to step foot on the campus.

To add to the problems, professors of Italian and Spanish went on strike, claiming there were not enough professors and courses. Another incident which caught public attention was the "crèche sauvage" or unapproved child-care center. A group of leftists thought that social justice required them to establish a child-care center in an annex of the university. They brought in approximately sixty small children, mostly from the surrounding "bidonvilles." Shortly after the center was set up—including the appropriate "revolutionary" murals on the walls—the municipal health authorities showed up. They told Ricoeur that the child-care center was a danger to the health of the children because there was inadequate sanitation, untrained workers, no proper food preparation areas, and so forth. They ordered him to shut it down. He had no power, short of calling the police, to force the leftists to leave and close the center.

Finally, many other faculty simply refused to come to the university to teach their classes, on the grounds that their personal security could not be guaranteed. In consultation with the University Council, Ricoeur decided to "banalize" the campus. This meant that the police could patrol the streets of the campus just as they patrol any other street. They still could not enter any of the university buildings unless specifically requested by the university officials to do so. Some time before, the police had already received the authority to patrol the campus at night, so this was a change only for the daytime. It was on February 26 that Ricoeur and Rémond went to the minister of education, Olivier Guichard, to discuss their and the council's recommendation to banalize the campus.

The very next day, the municipal police began circulating in patrol cars on the campus. Almost immediately, some Maoists began stoning the police cars. Then they erected barricades with tables, benches, and anything else they could find. When the police got out of their cars to remove the barricades, they were hit with stones, bottles, and sticks.

The next day, Saturday, February 28, the minister of the interior, Raymond Marcellin, met with the préfect of the police and representatives of the minister of education to discuss how to proceed with the banalization on Monday of the next week. Their decision was to use whatever force was required.

The week opened with continued clashes between the Maoists and the police, who were trying to establish their patrols on the streets of the university. The word was out and leftists from all over Paris came to Nanterre to join in the battle. By Tuesday, there was a pitched battle between the leftist students and the police. The police had arrived in large numbers, wearing riot gear and carrying shields. They massed outside of the buildings, while the students were inside, mostly on the upper floors. The students rained down on the police a constant barrage of chairs, typewriters, books, table legs, and any other objects they could get through the windows. For their part, the police were shooting tear gas grenades through the windows and hurling rocks and other objects back at the students.

36

The police brought in a bulldozer to demolish some of the barricades. A student picked up a tear gas grenade and threw it into the cab of the bulldozer as it went across the campus. It went out of control and wrecked several police vehicles, scattering police everywhere. At this point, some of the leftists came out of the buildings, and there were running battles with the police. Totally frustrated at this point, some of the police had the idea of punishing the students by vandalizing their cars in the parking lot. Virtually every car had its tires slashed, windows broken, and body panels dented. One sociologist said, "It's May in reverse; now its the police demolishing cars."[39] At this point, sixty police had been injured. The municipal police chased many of the demonstrators into the university restaurant. They threw tear gas inside, smashed the windows, and then beat with nightsticks and rocks those who came stumbling out. The demonstrators mingled with approximately 400 students who were not involved, but who were simply eating dinner in the cafeteria. The police then waded into the mass of students and begin savagely beating them indiscriminately. The police were out of hand in their rage, and their officers could not control them. Finally, the national Gendarmes had to intervene to protect the students from the municipal police who, at this point, had gone berserk.

By Wednesday, an unusual spring snow storm covered the campus and blew into the buildings through the broken windows. Many students had been trapped in the buildings by the events, and Ricoeur and Rémond now were able to get the police to permit many of them to leave. Almost simultaneously, students left and police were withdrawn. The new campus was left in a shambles, with hundreds of thousands of dollars of damage to both the exterior and the interior of the buildings. Within a week, the classes resumed and the cleanup began.

On March 1 Paul Ricoeur had decided to resign, and, in the middle of the afternoon, called René Rémond to tell him this. They decided to keep it secret so as not to aggravate the tense situation. The pitched battle between the leftists and the police ended on March 4. Ricoeur informed the university council of his intentions on the ninth, and his resignation became effective on March 16, 1970. In his letter of resignation to the minister of education, Ricoeur gave as the principal reason his failing health. He also said that he could not perform his duties as doyen without neglecting his students and his courses. He added that the universities today face an insoluble problem, that of collective crime. It is possible to call the police on campus to stop or to investigate a theft, an assault, a rape, or other individual crime, or to make an arrest, but the university and the police seem powerless against collective crimes such as those witnessed at Nanterre. He said these can only be resolved by political means. He wrote bitterly of the decep-

---

39. *Express,* no. 974, 9–15 March 1970, 42.

tion he felt when the police were sent to the campus the day after he had called for banalization. He felt the action of the minister was provocative and was meant to weaken him while at the same time to serve as an excuse to attack the small bands of leftists still occupying the campus. He was especially unhappy that there had been no consultation and no planning before the police were sent to the campus. Ricoeur finished by saying that if only the universities had maintained the initiative of innovation and had changed more rapidly in the direction outlined in the Loi d'orientation, then the university would have been stronger and less susceptible to such attacks. He said, "At Nanterre we have lived, with disappointment and sometimes anger, with this incomprehensible policy of procrastination."[40] Indeed, this was the letter of a demoralized man, deceived by the minister, abandoned by his colleagues, who felt that his own personal attempt to lead and change the university by appeal to reason and imagination had failed.

The minister, Oliver Guichard, wrote a sharply worded reply to Ricoeur's letter of resignation. He reviewed the long history of doyens calling the police to their campuses, while admitting that today there was a difference since the troublemakers now aim at destroying the society as a whole. That is why the law allows the university officials to decide when to call the police. He then rejected Ricoeur's claim that sending the police the next day was an intentional provocation. He asserted that Ricoeur and Rémond came to him in a state of alarm, saying they could no longer guarantee the security of their campus. It was the leftists, he continued, who the next week attacked the police. Admitting that the university was fragile and in need of reform, he rejected Ricoeur's claim that the reforms were moving too slowly, claiming that it is better to go slow and consult all of the interested parties than to move quickly on the ministerial level and have the reforms rejected by the students or the professors.

Réne Rémond has said that Ricoeur did not fail, that in fact, he was an excellent administrator. He believes that if Ricoeur had only held on a few more weeks, he would have been seen as the savior of Nanterre instead of the doyen forced to resign by the leftists. He says,

> Even though in all circumstances he did as his conscience commanded, Paul Ricoeur, in resigning a responsibility he accepted only out of duty, had without doubt the feeling that he had failed. This impression is unjust and inaccurate: I have the sense that, if only a little extra resistance had allowed him to overcome the trial of the moment, and to hold on for several more weeks, the situation would

40. *Le Monde*, 18 March 1970, 16. Both Paul Ricoeur's letter of resignation and Mr. Guichard's response are printed under the headline "The Minister of National Education has accepted the resignation of Doyen Ricoeur."

have been reversed, in our favor this time, and he would have received the fruit of his patience and of the justness of his views.[41]

Paul Ricoeur then requested a three-year leave from the French university system. During these years, he taught at the University of Louvain and at the University of Chicago, from which he had received an honorary doctorate in the spring of 1967.

At about the same time as he was elected doyen at Nanterre, Paul put the finishing touches on a collection of his articles, published later that year as *The Conflict of Interpretations*.[42] All of these articles, which span the 1960s, had been previously published in some form, the first in 1961 and the latest in 1969, although a number of them were reworked for this collection. As a consequence, the reader can see clearly the development of Ricoeur's thought from the beginning to the end of the decade. Most importantly, we can see the shift in the intellectual scene in France, as he broadens his idea of hermeneutics from the interpretation of symbols or, "double-meaning expressions," to the interpretation of texts, and text-like works, including dreams, symptoms, monuments, and culture itself. Then, too, there is the constant battle with structuralism, as it took hold in France and became generalized from a method in the social sciences to a philosophical ideology.

In a post-phenomenological age, hermeneutics and structuralism were the philosophical successors to Husserl. In the lead article of the collection, "Existence and Hermeneutics,"[43] Ricoeur explains how his hermeneutics differs from Heidegger's ontology of understanding and tells us why he chose another path. In the group of articles on "Hermeneutics and Structuralism," he explains how his hermeneutics developed out of Husserl's original concern with meaning and how it differs from his previous phenomenology. He then argues that structuralism as an explanatory method is a powerful and legitimate approach to understanding social relationships, especially as used by the anthropologist Claude Levi-Strauss. He objects to it when it is elevated into a set of general philosophical presuppositions which claim exclusiveness as method, totality in extension,

41. René Rémond, *La Règle et le consentement* (Paris: Fayard, 1979): 119. Also, interview with René Rémond June 6, 1980, in Paris.

42. Paul Ricoeur, *Le Conflit des interprétations. Essais d'herméneutique* (Paris: Éditions du Seuil, 1969). In English as *The Conflict of Interpretations. Essays in Hermeneutics*, several translators with introduction by Don Ihde (Evanston: Northwestern University Press, 1974).

43. Paul Ricoeur, "Existence et herméneutique," *Interpretation der Welt*, ed. H. Kuhn, H. Kahlefeld, and K. Forster (Würzburg: Im Echter-Verlag, 1965). Reprinted in *Le Conflit des interprétations*. In English as "Existence and Hermeneutics," *The Conflict of Interpretations*, trans. Kathleen McLaughlin, 3–24.

and world as a closed system. This section ends with his well-known article "Structure, Word, Event,"[44] in which he clearly distinguishes his hermeneutics from the structuralism of Levi-Strauss. This article was first published in *Esprit* in 1967 in a special issue devoted to structuralism and its critics. After the article, there is a splendid debate between Ricoeur and Levi-Strauss, which shows, at once, the high respect each had for the other, and the unbridgeable gulf between their philosophical positions.

The next set of articles, "Hermeneutics and Psychoanalysis," deals with various aspects of Ricoeur's interpretation of Freud, such as the role of psychoanalysis in contemporary culture, as a part of that culture and as a method of interpreting culture. In an especially important article, "Technique and Nontechnique in Interpretation,"[45] Ricoeur sets out the place of the therapeutic technique in psychoanalysis, a technique which is independent from the method of investigation and the speculative theory. Then, he foreshadows one of the central claims in his book on Freud, that is, that psychoanalysis is not an observational or natural science, but a hermeneutical science. It deals with meanings, not facts, and it proceeds like a detective searching out clues in its attempt to understand the meaning of neurotic symptoms or dreams.

Another section of this book deals with the relation between hermeneutics and phenomenology and the symbolism of evil. This section groups articles which reiterate and extend the theses of the *Symbolism of Evil*. In the final section, "Religion and Faith," Ricoeur gives a philosophical analysis of guilt, of the symbol of the father, and of the relationship between "Religion, Atheism, and Faith." This is the title of a two-part lecture he gave at Columbia University in 1966. These talks were in a series called the Bampton Lectures and were published in the United States as *The Religious Significance of Atheism*.[46] Several lectures given at another time in this series by Alasdair MacIntyre were also included in the book.

If one path from the *Symbolism of Evil* led to Ricoeur's broadening of his hermeneutics to include psychoanalytic interpretation, the other path led to his

44. Paul Ricoeur, "La structure, le mot, l'événement," *Esprit* 35, May (1967), 5, 801–21. Reprinted in *Le Conflit des interprétations*. In English as "Structure, Word, Event," *The Conflict of Interpretations*, trans. Robert Sweeney, 79–96.

45. Paul Ricoeur, "Technique et non-technique dans l'interprétation," *Archivio di Filosofia*, Atti del Colloquio internazionale, Roma, 1964, 1–2, pp. 23–37. Reprinted in *Le Conflit des interprétations*. In English as "Technique and Non-Technique in Interpretation," reprinted in *The Conflict of Interpretations*, trans. Willis Domingo, 177–95.

46. Paul Ricoeur, "Religion, Atheism and Faith" (Bampton Lectures in America, delivered at Columbia Unviersity, 1966), in *The Religious Significance of Atheism*, ed. Alasdair MacIntyre and Paul Ricoeur (New York: Columbia University Press, 1969). Reprinted in *The Conflict of Interpretations*, 440–67.

careful reading of the principal Protestant theologians of this century, including Barth, Bultmann, and others. In particular, Ricoeur was interested in a philosophical interpretation of certain themes or concepts such as "accusation," "consolation," "testimony," "guilt," and so forth. He was also interested in bringing to bear the methods of contemporary language analysis and hermeneutics on the question of the meaning of religious language. These investigations took place alongside his interests in creativity in language, particularly in metaphor.

When Ricoeur took a three-year leave from the University of Paris X-Nanterre, as it is now called, he began, in reality, a fifteen-year self-imposed exile from the French intellectual life. Most of his articles were published either in English or, if in French, they were published outside of France. When he left France for Belgium and the United States, he became better and better known all over the world and, incredibly, virtually forgotten in France.

His first course after leaving Nanterre was at the Catholic University of Louvain, at a time of civil strife between the Flemish-speaking and the French-speaking communities in Belgium. During his three years of teaching there, his courses were entitled, "The Semantics of Action," "Course on Hermeneutics," and "The Discourse of Action." These courses were not published, except in mimeographed form. In 1975, he returned to Paris and gave a graduate-level seminar on "The Semantics of Action." This seminar has been published in a book of the same name.[47]

During the three years of his leave, Ricoeur taught at the University of Chicago in the early fall and in the spring and spent the winter term commuting from Chatenay Malabry to Louvain each week to give his course there.

The American Years

AT THE UNIVERSITY OF CHICAGO, Paul held the John Nuveen Chair in the Divinity School, although his appointment was jointly in the Department of Philosophy and the Committee on Social Thought, a multidisciplinary degree-granting program to which a number of departments contributed. He was the successor to Paul Tillich, the famous Protestant theologian.

One of the main reasons Paul and Simone agreed to go to Chicago each year—and sometimes for two terms a year—was Mircea Eliade and his wife, Christinel. Paul met Mircea, a refugee from Romania, when he was teaching at the University of Strasbourg. Eliade had been called to the Sewell L. Avery chair in the Divinity school in the early 1960s. They had been friends in Strasbourg, in Paris, and now in Chicago. Christinel was a frequent companion of Simone's and Mircea and Paul jointly taught some courses in the Divinity School.

47. Paul Ricoeur, *La Sémantique de l'action* (Paris: Éditions du Centre National de la recherche scientifique, 1977).

Other very close friends in Chicago were André and Claire Lacocque, originally from Belgium. André is a professor at the Chicago Theological Seminary and is an expert on the Old Testament. Claire teaches French at the University of Chicago Lab School. During the first few years that the Ricoeurs came to Chicago, they rented furnished apartments near the university, frequently in the same building or apartment complex as the Lacocques. Later, the Lacocques bought a very large apartment in a high-rise building near Chicago's Museum of Science and Industry, only a few blocks from the university and just across the street from Lake Michigan. The Ricoeurs, then coming for only one term per year, would stay with the Lacocques. This was especially comfortable for Simone, who spoke very little English—although, I must add, she has infinite patience with others' French, no matter how slow or how poorly spoken.

During the entire decade of the 1970s, whenever the Ricoeurs were in America, Paul was invited to give lectures at universities all over the country, and Simone frequently accompanied him. His great disappointment with the events at Nanterre was counterbalanced by the honors he began to receive all over the world. In 1970, for example, he received honorary doctorates from Nimegen (Netherlands) and from Ohio University. These had been preceded by honorary doctorates at Bâle, Chicago, and Montréal in the 1960s. They were followed in quick succession by honorary doctorates at DePaul, Zurich, Boston College, Louvain, Seabury Western Theological Seminary (Evanston), Toronto, Copenhagen, Duquesne (Pittsburgh), Columbia, Tilburg, Ottawa, Buenos Aires, and McGill (Montreal).

In addition to giving courses on hermeneutics, with close attention to the semantics of action, Ricoeur was preparing his book on metaphor. His longtime interest in symbolic language led him to a fascination with creativity in language, especially metaphoric, symbolic, and narrative language. His research on metaphor began showing up as early as February of 1972, in an article translated as "Metaphor and the Main Problem of Hermeneutics."[48] His thesis involves linking the interpretation of texts with the understanding of metaphors: "To what extent may we treat metaphor as a work in miniature? The answer to this first question will help us afterwards to raise the second question: To what extent may the hermeneutical problem of text interpretation be considered as a large-scale

48. Paul Ricoeur, "La métaphore et le problème central de l'herméneutique," *Revue philosophique de Louvain* 70, (1972), February, 93–112. Reprinted in English as "Metaphor and the Main Problem of Hermeneutics," *New Literary History* 6, (1974–75): 95–110. Also reprinted in *The Philosophy of Paul Ricoeur*, ed. Charles Reagan and David Stewart (Boston: Beacon Press, 1978): 134-48. Also translated as "Metaphor and the Central Problem of Hermeneutics," in Paul Ricoeur, *Hermeneutics and the Human Sciences*, ed. and trans. John B. Thompson (Cambridge: Cambridge University Press, 1981): 165–81.

expansion of the problems condensed in the explication of a local metaphor in a given text?"[49] In this article, he gives a glimpse of the main conclusion of his book on metaphor: Metaphors give us a new way to describe, a redescription, of the world, just as the interpretation of texts presents to us a world which could be our world, and, to use Gadamer's phrase, creates a "fusion of horizons" of the world in which I live and the world in which I *could* live.

Ricoeur's book *The Rule of Metaphor*[50] is an interesting collection of eight semi-autonomous studies of which the first six are mostly careful expositions and critiques of historical and contemporary Anglo-Saxon and French theories of metaphor. The seventh study, "Metaphor and Reference," is the most important chapter in the book since it is here that Ricoeur establishes his main thesis that metaphor is a way of redescribing the world and that, therefore, poetic language has a referent. In short, if a metaphor destroys the possibility of a literal meaning, it also destroys the possibility of a referent for the sentence. But this opens up the possibility that metaphorical meaning creates a new referent, a new world of the text.

If metaphorical sentences and poetic works have some sort of referent, Ricoeur is constrained to answer both the epistemological question of metaphorical *truth* and the ontological question about what is, that is, *reality*. In response to the first question, Ricoeur says, "the comparison of model and metaphor at least shows us the direction: as the conjunction of fiction and redescription suggests, poetic feeling itself also develops an experience of reality in which invention and discovery cease being opposed and where creation and revelation coincide."[51] The closest we get to an answer to the ontological question is in the final essay, entitled "Metaphor and Philosophical Discourse." In this very long and very difficult study, Ricoeur sets himself to show the relation between speculative (philosophical) discourse and poetic language. He thoroughly criticizes Derrida's "White Mythology"[52] and rejects his claim that certain metaphors—for example, heliotropic ones—are essential to Western metaphysics. Ricoeur argues that there is no necessary connection between any particular metaphors and any particular metaphysics.

49. Paul Ricoeur, "Metaphor and the Main Problem of Hermeneutics," in *The Philosophy of Paul Ricoeur*, 136.

50. Paul Ricoeur, *The Rule of Metaphor. Multi-Disciplinary Studies of the Creation of Meaning in Language*, trans. R. Czerny with K. McLaughlin and J. Costello (Toronto: University of Toronto Press, 1977, and London: Routledge and Kegan Paul, 1978). The French version was published as *La Métaphore vive* (Paris: Éditions du Seuil, 1975).

51. *The Rule of Metaphor*, 246.

52. Jacques Derrida, "White Mythology: Metaphor in the Text of Philosophy," *New Literary History*, trans. F .C .T. Moore, 6, Autumn (1974), 1, 5–74. Originally published as "La mythologie blanche," *Poétique* 5 (1971).

This book was the first major work Ricoeur published in France since the debacle at Nanterre. Its reception was a sign of the nearly total eclipse of this once-famous philosopher in his native land. There were only a few reviews of the book in France, and they were mostly negative. French reviewers were puzzled by Ricoeur's careful attention to so many British and American writers and were not at all sympathetic to his criticism of Jacques Derrida, who, by this time, was one of the philosophical stars of the French intelligentsia. On the other hand, when the English translation was published only two years later, it was widely and very favorably reviewed. Indeed, Paul Ricoeur had become one of the best-known philosophers in the English-speaking world. Most reviewers, even critics, were astounded by Ricoeur's encyclopedic knowledge of theories of metaphor and the fact that he was fully conversant with all of the contemporary theorists on both the Continent and in the Anglo-Saxon world.

In 1977, Ricoeur took a long lecture trip to Japan, his first visit to that country. Several of his books had been translated into Japanese and he found a large audience at each of the universities where he spoke. He maintained, of course, his intense visiting lecture schedule in the United States. In 1978, he was elected as a foreign member of the American Academy of Arts and Sciences. In 1979, he gave the prestigious Zaharoff Lecture at Oxford. This 65-page lecture was published as *The Contribution of French Historiography to the Theory of History*.[53] Like many of his articles during this period, it was not published in France. Nevertheless, this, and other articles were the result of research he was doing for his three-volume work *Time and Narrative*, which would be published in the early to mid-eighties.

In 1979, Ricoeur's seminar in Paris was devoted to studies of narrative. This seminar was held at the Husserl Archives (Husserl Library), a branch of the Centre National de la Recherche Scientifique, of which Ricoeur was the director. The archive was a small library and office suite containing a large number of copies of Husserl's papers (the originals were held in the Husserl Archives in Louvain) and secondary sources on phenomenology. The Husserl Archives supported several graduate students and one or two full-time researchers. The seminar was on the advanced level and was attended mainly by foreign professors and graduate students. Paul gave the first three or four lectures and then the students presented their research papers on the topic chosen for that year. The topics were frequently the ones on which Ricoeur was working at the time, and his lectures were early versions of chapters of books or major articles which

53. Paul Ricoeur, *The Contribution of French Historiography to the Theory of History*, The Zaharoff Lecture for 1978–79 (Oxford: Clarendon Press, 1980, and New York: Oxford University Press, 1980).

would appear a few years later. During the late 1970s and the early 1980s, these seminars prefigured the themes and topics of *Time and Narrative*.

On February 27, 1978, Ricoeur celebrated his sixty-fifth birthday. This event is worth noting because the number of books and papers he has written after this point, the usual time of retirement, is truly astonishing. In 1980, he retired from the University of Paris-Nanterre. He continued to teach one or two quarters a year at the University of Chicago until 1991, when he accepted the title of John Nuveen Professor Emeritus. As the reader will see, even after ending his academic career, he continued publishing books and articles and presenting papers at philosophical conferences.

In the transitional period between *The Rule of Metaphor* and the publication of *Time and Narrative*, Ricoeur's interests shifted from the hermeneutics of symbols and texts towards a philosophical analysis of creativity in language. In particular, "narrativity" and the narrative, whether fictional or historical, became the focus of his interest in texts, as opposed to symbols and metaphors. Second, he returned to his fascination with human action, going back to the philosophy of the will, but this time aided by the powerful techniques of Anglo-American analytical philosophy. Third, he took up once again the philosophical problem of time. He had taught courses, especially at the Sorbonne, on the concept of "time" and the long history of philosophical attempts to understand time. Narrative, action, and time are the unifying concepts in *Time and Narrative*.

During the 1970s, Ricoeur wrote three especially important articles which progressively developed his thought in these three areas. The 1971 article, "The Model of the Text,"[54] is an essay on how human action resembles texts in a number of important features, and he suggests that we could use the techniques of understanding texts, particularly the rules and techniques of hermeneutics, to understand human actions, both individual actions and the actions of groups. This article has been widely reprinted and generated a great deal of discussion in the social sciences in England and the United States.

The second transitional article is "Explanation and Understanding: On Some Remarkable Connections Among the Theory of Text, Theory of Action, and Theory of History."[55] Here Ricoeur briefly discusses the dialectic between expla-

54. Paul Ricoeur, "The Model of the Text: Meaningful Action Considered as a Text," *Social Research* 38, Fall (1971), 3, 529–62.

55. Paul Ricoeur, "Expliquer et comprendre. Sur quelques connexions remarquable entre la théorie du texte, la théorie de l'action et la théorie de l'histoire," *Revue philosophique de Louvain* 75, February (1977), 1, 126–47. In English as "Explanation and Understanding: On Some Remarkable Connections among the Theory of Text, Theory of Action and Theory of History," trans. Charles E. Reagan and David Stewart in *The Philosophy of Paul Ricoeur. An Anthology of His Work*, ed. Charles E. Reagan and David Stewart (Boston: Beacon Press, 1978): 149–66.

nation and understanding, two activities which Dilthey thought were diametrically opposed. Ricoeur's basic claim is that there is a dialectic, not a dichotomy, between explanation and understanding such that understanding is the goal of explanation and explanation is the means to understanding. He then shows how in the theory of the text explanation is required because the text has an independence from its author, its original audience, and has an independence from the actual situation of speaking. On the other hand, the goal of all explanatory models, structuralist or otherwise, is understanding. There is the same dialectic in the theory of action between explanation in the sense of causes of events and the understanding of intentions and motives of action. Finally, in historiography, Ricoeur claims that "history begins when we no longer have immediate understanding."[56] But understanding is what allows us, ultimately, to "follow the story." He says that the text is a good paradigm for human action, and human action is a referent for a whole category of texts, namely, historical texts.

Finally, in 1980, he published an article, "Narrative Time,"[57] in which he carefully analyzed the relation between time and narrative. He says, "In order to show the reciprocity between narrativity and temporality, I shall conduct this study as an analysis with two foci: for each feature of narrative brought out by reflection on either history or fictional narrative, I shall attempt to find a corresponding feature of temporality brought out by an existential analysis of time."[58] Each of these articles was preparatory to Ricoeur's next major work, the three volumes of *Time and Narrative*, a work which would be all-consuming for him from 1979 to 1985.

During this most productive period, Ricoeur settled into an annual cadence: Christmas in Paris, lectures in Europe, spring term (March to May) in Chicago, late May and early June in Italy (Naples and Rome), July and August at his country home in Brittany, and a fall of intensive reading, writing, and lecturing in Europe.

In the summers of 1983, 1985, and 1994 he was invited to a most remarkable event. In August of each of those years, Pope John Paul II invited Ricoeur, along with a small group of other intellectuals, to join him for several days in the papal summer retreat at Castel Gandolfo outside of Rome. The days were spent in conversation, with each person invited to give a presentation, followed by long discussions.

In February of 1983, Paul and Simone, along with his longtime friend and

---

56. Cf. *The Philosophy of Paul Ricoeur. An Anthology of his Work*, 162.

57. Paul Ricoeur, "Narrative Time," *Critical Enquiry* (On Narrative), 7, Autumn (1980), 1, 169–90. Abridged translation of "La fonction narrative et l'expérience humaine du temps," *Archivio di Filosofia* (esistenza, mito, ermeneutica. Scritti per Enrico Castelli. I), 80, (1980), 1, 343–67.

58. "Narrative Time," 170.

editor, François Wahl, and other guests, celebrated the publication of the first volume of *Time and Narrative*.[59] The entire work is divided into four parts, with Volume 1 containing two parts and each of the other two volumes one part each. Part I is composed of relatively independent studies of time according to St. Augustine and the function of emplotment according to Aristotle, joined by a remarkable study of "mimesis" where Ricoeur lays out his own analysis of time and narrative. Part II begins with an account of the attack on narrative in history by French historiographers and by the logical positivists. In the second chapter, he presents arguments against the positivists and in favor of the place of narrative in history. In the final chapter, he argues for his thesis that there is and must be a derivative connection between history and narrative such that history at once remains a science and retains its bonds with our competence to follow a story. In short, in volume 1, Ricoeur develops a theory of narrative and tests it against the narratives of history.

In Part III (in volume 2), Ricoeur tests his theory of the triple "mimesis" on fictional narratives. In a chapter on "The Metamorphoses of Plot," he explores the limits of narrative. This is followed by a chapter on the semiotics of narrative, in which he discusses the theories of Propp, Bremond, and Greimas. Next, in a chapter entitled "Playing with Time," he explores the grammar of narrative and time. Finally, he illustrates his thesis with a chapter on three famous novels dominated by time: Woolf's *Mrs. Dalloway,* Mann's *The Magic Mountain,* and Proust's *Remembrance of Things Past.*

In Part IV (volume 3), he begins with a study on "The Aporias of Temporality," in which he takes up the debate between St. Augustine and Aristotle, between Kant and Husserl, and between Heidegger and "metaphysics" on the nature of time. Then he devotes a chapter to "The Refiguration of Time by History," in which he examines the relation between the experience of time and the time of nature, the reality of the historical past, and then argues against Hegel's view of historical time. He finishes this chapter with a section on the hermeneutics of historical time. The third chapter is devoted to reading as a kind of mediation between the world of the text and the world of the reader. This chapter includes sections on imaginative variation in fictional narrative, the act of reading, and finishes with a section on the "crossed reference" between history and fiction.

This book shows clearly that Ricoeur is a master of the history of philosophy and that he is very well read in the secondary literature, in English, German, and

---

59. Paul Ricoeur, *Temps et récit I* (Paris: Le Seuil, 1983). *Temps et récit II. La configuration dans le récit de fiction* (Paris: Le Seuil, 1984). *Temps et récit III. Le temps raconté* (Paris: Le Seuil, 1985). In English as *Time and Narrative 1, 2, 3,* trans. Kathleen McLaughlin (Blamey) and David Pellauer (Chicago: University of Chicago Press, 1984, 1985, 1988).

French, on Aristotle and St. Augustine. He chooses masterpieces in all three of these languages to serve as examples of novels with time as a central theme. He demonstrates a command of both French and English-language historiography and literary theory. Very few of his readers have his breadth and depth of knowledge, a fact that left many reviewers puzzled and, in some cases, hostile. On the whole, the work was very well received in France and, when the translations were available a few years later, in the United States as well.

Return to France

THE PUBLICATION of this three-volume work led to the "rediscovery" of Paul Ricoeur in France. He burst back on the intellectual scene, with interviews in print and on television. His ability to combine historical figures in philosophy, such as Aristotle, St. Augustine, Kant, Hegel, and Heidegger, with the most contemporary of philosophical interests, such as narrative, action theory, and historiography, is a rare talent, greatly appreciated by French intellectuals. In addition, here was a philosopher who had published his first works in the days of Sartre, Merleau-Ponty, and Marcel, and now was still publishing major works after the deaths of Lacan and Foucault, after the eclipse of structuralism and the total demise of Lacanian psychoanalysis. In one sense he had outlasted his critics; in another, he had moved beyond them.

His standing in the philosophical world was rewarded with an invitation to give the famous Gifford Lectures in Scotland. Most of the year of 1985 was spent in preparation. He chose the theme of personal identity and the individual's relations to others. Each of his lectures would address some aspect of this general theme.

In the summer of 1985, August 14 to be precise, the Ricoeurs celebrated their fiftieth wedding anniversary at their country home in Préfailles. They were surrounded by their five grown-up children with their spouses, and their fourteen grandchildren, along with some family friends. It was a joyous occasion, marking fifty years of Paul and Simone's love and total dedication to each other. And, it came at a time when Paul was, once again, at the pinnacle of his renown in France. He was France's best-known philosopher—even in France.

The Gifford Lectures were given in late February and early March—February 20 to March 7—in 1986 in Edinburgh. During this period, his son Olivier transcribed his dictated lectures, and then Paul reworked the typewritten text Olivier prepared. His translator, Kathleen Blamey, then put them in English. Paul reworked the English version, shortening the lectures to fit the alloted time. This work went on until the very time the Ricoeurs left for Edinburgh.

Olivier came over to Edinburgh and spent five days with his parents and sat in on several of the lectures. He then returned to Paris. After the lectures were finished, Paul and Simone spent a few days touring in Scotland, and then returned to France. Later in the same day that they arrived in Paris, Paul left again to go to Prague, to visit some Czech philosophers who had lost their jobs in the university because of their opposition to the Communist government. The day after his arrival, he was notified of the tragic death of Olivier, who had committed suicide by jumping off the top of his apartment building to the street below. Paul rushed home from Prague and the Ricoeur family began a very long grieving process for Olivier. I will say much more about Olivier in the memoir, but even though this essay is about Paul Ricoeur, it is impossible to write about Paul without mentioning Olivier. In fact, in the middle of Chapter 9 in *Oneself as An Other*, there is an "Interlude" on tragic action dedicated to Olivier.

During the spring and summer of 1986, Paul was so grief-stricken that he could hardly work. His efforts to revise the Gifford Lectures came to a halt, although he did read revised versions of several chapters in Munich later that year. Much of the summer was spent at Préfailles revising and correcting the manuscript for a collection of his more recent articles. This collection was important for his French readers since many of the articles were written in English, or if they were published in French, they were published in Belgian or German philosophical journals. The title of this collection, *From Text to Action*,[60] is another sign of Ricoeur's philosophical interest turning from the hermeneutics of texts back towards the analysis of human action, one of the principal themes of his earlier "philosophical anthropology."

The most important articles in this collection, such as "The Model of the Text," and "Explanation and Understanding," have already been mentioned. In addition to the articles on hermeneutics and the relation between language and action, such as in "Imagination in Discourse and in Action," there is a section on "Ideology, Utopia, and Politics." This group of articles addresses the question of the critique of ideology and the relation between ideology and utopia as forms of social imagination. The collection as a whole ends with an analysis of the relation between ethics and politics. This concern is addressed in *Oneself as An Other*, and remains the central topic of his articles written in the early 1990s.

If is very difficult to give a brief account of *Oneself as An Other*,[61] and yet, once again, to the extent that Ricoeur's life is his work, I must try. (I give a longer, much more detailed account of this work in my "Philosophical Essay" in this book.) The title of Ricoeur's book indicates the principal themes: it is a re-

60. Paul Ricoeur, *From Text to Action. Essays in Hermeneutics, 2*, trans. Kathleen Blamey and John B. Thompson (Evanston: Northwestern University Press, 1991). Translation of *Du texte à l'action. Essais d'herméneutique, II* (Paris: Éditions du Seuil, 1986).

61. Paul Ricoeur, *Oneself as Another*, trans. Kathleen Blamey (Chicago: University of Chicago Press, 1992). Translation of *Soi-même comme un autre* (Paris: Éditions du Seuil, 1990).

flection on the self or subject, a dialectic on the meaning of the word "same" in the sense of identical or in the sense of one and the same, and, finally, a dialectic between the self and the other. The first group of studies, Chapters 1 and 2, is based on a *philosophy of language,* both as semantics and as pragmatics. This analytic stage is made necessary by the indirect status of the self. Hermeneutics is always a philosophy of detour; the hermeneutics of the self must take a detour through the analysis of the language in which we talk about the self. This analysis is lead by the question "Who?" Who speaks? Who acts? Whose story is told? Who is responsible?

The second group, Chapters 3 and 4, is based on a *philosophy of action* in the sense this has taken in analytic philosophy. The interest here is in language about action and in speech acts where the agent of an action designates himself as the one who acts. Ricoeur reminds us that these long analytic forays are "characteristic of the indirect style of a hermeneutics of the self, in stark contrast to the demand for immediacy belonging to the cogito."[62]

The third group, Chapters 5 and 6, is centered on the question of *personal identity.* It is in these chapters that Ricoeur tries to solve some of the aporias of personal identity by distinguishing between two senses of identity: identity as sameness and identity as selfhood. The latter concept explains how there can be an identity over time, such as in promise-making. I am the same person who made the promise twenty years ago who is now bound to keep it, even though there are few similarities (identity-sameness) left.

The fourth group, Chapters 7, 8, and 9, make another detour through the ethical and moral determinations of action. This group represents Ricoeur's "metaphysic of morals," in that he distinguishes a teleological ethics, "live the good life with and for others in just institutions," from the deontological moral rules which serve as guides to the application of the fundamental rule to particular situations. In short, he sets up a dialectic between Aristotle and Kant, in which Kant provides the practical application of the Aristotelian principle and Aristotle provides the ultimate justification for a deontology of maxims. The most important thread which winds throughout these chapters is that the self, as a moral being, is constituted in the face of the other, who says, "Do not kill me, do not steal from me. . . ." It is "practical wisdom" which is the third term in the dialectic, mediating between the aporias that arise when we try to apply the moral rules to particular cases and the teleological desire to live the good life with and for others in just institutions.

The publication of this book in March of 1990 was not only a philosophical triumph for Paul Ricoeur, but it put a sense of closure on his mourning for Oliv-

---

62. *Oneself as Another,* 17.

ier. In the spring of 1991, he won the prize in philosophy from the Académie Française, a major award worth almost $10,000, to say nothing of the prestige.

This is not the end of the story. The story does not have an ending, especially when it is a biographical narrative of the life of a man who is still living, still writing, still lecturing. In the last several years, Ricoeur has kept up his pace in the publication of articles, mostly on the theories of justice of John Rawls and others and on the relation between ethics and politics. In the fall of 1995, he published two shorter books, one, entitled, *Réflections accomplies*, contains his "Intellectual Autobiography," along with several articles. The other, called *Justice*, is a collection of his recent articles on justice and its application in the modern world. His "rediscovery" in France is evidenced by the numerous interviews on television and in the newspapers. He was invited by President Mitterand to attend a state dinner at the Elysée Palace in honor of President and Mrs. Clinton in June of 1994. And yet, his greatest joy is still his summer at Préfailles, working on his next paper and taking long walks along the beautiful coast of Brittany.

• 2 •

MEMOIR

As Paul Ricoeur himself says, there are many ways to configure the temporality in a narrative, but I have chosen a chronological order, the historical order, in keeping with my goal of presenting a biography of Paul Ricoeur. In the biographical essay of chapter 1 above, the chronology was Paul's life and work; in this essay, it is guided by the passage of my relation with him. My goal there was sketch the main lines of his life and his work. In it, I restricted myself to writing on events and works that are all documented in books, articles, newspaper interviews and accounts, and other forms of evidence appropriate to the historian. In this essay, I want to fill in some of the blank spaces in the picture by relying on my own experiences as a student, colleague, and friend of Paul Ricoeur for over thirty years. I will rely heavily on my notes from conversations we have had over the years. In this sense, the memoir is very personal, while the biographical essay could have been written by someone who had never known Ricoeur personally.

I met Paul Ricoeur in November of 1962 when I was a student at the Institut d'études européennes (Institute of European Studies) in Paris. This institute is a study-abroad program for American students. It made all of the travel and housing arrangements, provided an intensive French course for six weeks before the beginning of the academic year, and arranged for some courses to be taught by French professors at the institute. Most students took the majority of their courses at the Sorbonne, the Institute for Political Science, the Catholic Institute, or other universities, institutes, or centers.

Paul Ricoeur was a philosophy teacher for us, as were Henri Birault and Jean Wahl. This was a very distinguished group of professors from the Sorbonne (some would say they were wasted on the young Americans). Paul Ricoeur was reaching the peak of his renown at the Sorbonne and was a major figure on the French intellectual scene. His course that year was on the "Concept of Time." He began with a historical review of what philosophers had said about time, from Plato and Aristotle to Kant and Husserl. After each historical account, he would tell us which problems of time were apparently solved by that philosopher and which ones remained—and which were aggravated by that philosopher's position. It is ironic now to think that I sat in on Ricoeur's first research and teaching on a concept that would occupy—and preoccupy—him from then on.

All of us took other courses, mostly at the Sorbonne. I took several philosophy courses there. There was a stark difference between the two places: At the institute, the classes were small, the professor showed personal interest in his students, and we had homework and tests throughout the year. In the pre-1968 Sorbonne, overflowing with students, none of these things occurred. I was especially impressed that Ricoeur asked each of us to pronounce our name as he called the roll. From that point on, he addressed each of us by our surname. I also remember that he was never short or condescending in answering our naive questions or impatient at our slowness in understanding difficult things, such as Kant's "forms of time and space." It is Paul Ricoeur and that class, I believe, that converted me to an academic career and provided me with a model for teaching philosophy.

As that year drew to a close, I bought the first two volumes of "The Philosophy of the Will" and asked him to autograph them for me. His salutation was very complimentary, and five years later I was drawn back to *Le Volontaire et l'involontaire* (later translated as *Freedom and Nature*) as the principal subject of my doctoral thesis. After I finished my degree and obtained a teaching job, my philosophical interests turned elsewhere.

About five years later, in the spring of 1973, I heard that Paul would be giving some lectures at the University of Oklahoma. I went there and we reestablished our acquaintance. I learned that he was then teaching each year at the University of Chicago, and I invited him to give a lecture at my university. In the fall of 1973 he came to Manhattan, Kansas. At that time, I paid no attention to sports, so I was dismayed to learn that there were no hotel rooms available because of Saturday's football game. So, Paul would have to stay at my house. My wife and I worried a great deal about having such a famous person in our home, especially since we had no living room furniture. (No need to recount the story of a young professor starting a family and job almost simultaneously . . . we all went through it.) Needless to say, Paul was a most gracious guest and his warm personality and gentle ways soon put us at ease. I discussed with him my plans for my sabbatical in Paris the next year, and he offered to let us stay in his house in Chatenay-Malabry, a suburb south of Paris, during the fall and again for two months in the spring, while he was at the University of Chicago. This offer was the beginning of the experiences which made writing this chapter—and probably this book— possible.

In the fall of 1974, my wife, my twenty-month-old son, and I went to Chatenay to live in the Ricoeur's apartment at Les Murs Blancs. Paul and Simone met us at the gate and helped us with our bags. Simone showed Sharon the house. Before he and Simone left for the airport, Paul and I took a long walk in the lovely gardens there and mostly discussed his book on metaphor. I remember him telling me that, after he had completed the book, he and his family went to

Greece for a brief holiday. He said that everywhere he went, he saw trucks with "Metaphora" painted on them. There was no escape from the philosophical theme which had dominated his life for the preceding three years. Then he realized that "Metaphora" literally meant "moving truck." Our orientation to the house, Les Murs Blancs, and Chatenay lasted about two hours. As a consequence, we had a great adventure in all respects.

The day after we moved in, we met Olivier, the Ricoeur's fourth child, born in 1947 and so twenty-seven years old at the time. This was the beginning of a twelve-year friendship which ended with Olivier's death in 1986. Olivier lived in two rooms in a lower level of the house. He was working for a large publishing house, Gallimard, and so was rarely around during the week. On weekends, we had two rituals: On Friday evenings, he would come up for a couple of hours and we would have a conversation, but the rule was that any time I made a grammatical mistake in French or used an inappropriate word, we would stop and he would correct me, explaining the grammatical rule or giving me a better choice of words. Second, he ate many Sunday dinners with us. He was also our principal advisor about practical things such as local transportation or where to buy what, and was helpful in every way.

Ricoeur's second son, Marc, was living in Paris at that time and I met him early on. The hot-water tank leaked, and so did the bathroom window every time it rained. Marc helped me to resolve both of those problems. During the course of that year, I got to know Marc and his wife, Suzanne, and their children.

Paul and Simone returned in December and reclaimed their house. We moved to Paris to an apartment. In January, I began attending Ricoeur's advanced seminar, held in the Husserl Archives on rue Parmentier. This seminar lasted three months. The students were about evenly divided between French graduate students and young professors in the lycée and foreign graduate students and professors. The course began with a "vin d'honneur" which was purely a social event at which the students became acquainted.

At the first class, Paul gave an outline of the course, that year devoted to "The Semantics of Action," a set of problems at the intersection of the philosophy of language and the philosophy of action. It was, as he said, a return to the questions about human action which intrigued him in his "Philosophy of the Will," but now he was armed with the analytical techniques of Anglo-American linguistic philosophy. He had begun his new work on this topic the previous year at Louvain. Each lecture lasted an hour, and there was an hour for discussion. During this discussion period, he allowed those students who wanted to give presentations to choose from a list of topics and authors. After his series of lectures was finished, one or two of the students gave a presentation at each class, followed by discussion. So this was my return to a class in which Paul Ricoeur was the

Paul Ricoeur and his sister, Alice, in 1916.

Alice Ricoeur in 1929.

Adèle Ricoeur, Paul's aunt, in 1929.

Paul in scout uniform in 1929.

Paul Ricoeur in 1932.

Paul and Simone Ricoeur on their wedding day, 1935.

Paul and Simone with their sons Jean-Paul and Marc at Préfailles, 1939.

Postcard from the Swiss Red Cross notifying Simone that Paul was alive
in a POW camp, June 26, 1940.

Paul (second from right) with other prisoners of war at Oflag IID,
near Gross Born, Germany, in 1942

Paul with Gabriel Marcel at Cerisy in 1955.

professor. It was interesting that twelve years later and at a much advanced course-level, Ricoeur's gentle and friendly spirit animated the class, and the self-conscious polemic which frequently spoils philosophical discussions was completely absent.

A year and a half later, we had the opportunity to return to France for a year, during which I was a Fulbright visiting professor at the University of Toulouse. We spent the month of September, once again, in the Ricoeurs' house. Olivier was happy to see us, and we continued our friendship just as before, with Olivier a frequent dinner guest. At Christmas we came back to Chatenay where we borrowed the apartment of Michel and Françoise Winock, who lived on the third floor of the same building as the Ricoeurs. One particularly joyous occasion was the family Christmas dinner, to which my wife and I were invited. The already large dining-room table was doubled in length with the addition of two smaller tables. In addition to Olivier and two of his friends, the Ricoeurs' daughter, Noëlle, and their son Etienne and his wife were present. Everyone helped with the preparation and it was an excellent Christmas dinner. The conversation was animated and lasted long into the night.

Several months later, I had the occasion to dine with the Ricoeurs and their oldest son, Jean-Paul, a practicing psychiatrist living in Marseilles. He was a Lacanian through and through. Jean-Paul was studying with Lacan at the time that Paul was attending Lacan's seminars and writing his book on Freud. They had had severe differences in their reading of Freud and their appreciation for Jacques Lacan. At the time of this dinner, the definitive break between Lacan and Ricoeur was thirteen years in the past. It was clear from the conversation that the passion of their differences had diminished considerably, mostly because Paul had moved beyond psychoanalysis and Freud and his hermeneutics was turning towards narrative. Our discussion centered on whether Lacanism was a cult of personality which would vanish after Lacan died. Jean-Paul also led me through some of the internecine battles within the Lacanian movement. Jean-Paul's wit and genuine humaneness mirrored that of his father.

There was a lapse of three years until my next visit to Chatenay, in late May of 1980. I stayed in a room in the carriage house at Les Murs Blancs, just across from the Ricoeurs' apartment. I got there a few days before Paul arrived. When he came, he invited me to sit with him on the bench beneath the large tree just in front of his apartment. I asked him about his health, since he had had some heart problems the previous November in Chicago. He told me that it was his arteries rather than his heart and that he was taking medication for it. He said that he needed to take long walks daily and asked me to join him.

We discussed the dissertation of his Irish friend, Richard Kearney, whom I met later at Cérisy-la-Salle. He was troubled by the "deconstructionist" theses of Derrida and Kearney's similar claims. Knowing about his serious health problems, I asked him if he ever thought of death. He said, "I have integrated the knowledge that I am not immortal into my life. You know, the two hardest things to accept are that you are going to die and that not everyone loves you. Nanterre and the Lacanians taught me that bitter lesson."

A few days later, we took a long walk in the Parc de Sceaux, a large, lovely formal park with a small chateau in one corner. The park itself is laid out much like Versailles, with a long canal, fountains, geometrical lawns, and wooded areas surrounding some of the paths. During this walk, I asked him about his military experience just before the Second World War. He told me of doing his year of obligatory military service just after passing his *agrégation*. Half of the year was at St. Cyr, the military school near Versailles, and the other half in his home unit, the 47th Infantry barracks in Rennes, in Brittany. He was recalled a couple of years later, in the winter of 1939. He said, "both the German and French armies were being mobilized. But with this important difference: The German army was being propagandized and incited and psychologically prepared for war, while the French army was being demoralized by inaction. This is always the advantage of ideological armies over those defending liberal democracies. This is the advantage Sparta had over Athens." I asked him if the French officers were well trained. He said, "Yes, but not for the kind of war they were going to have."

On our walk in the Parc de Sceaux the next day, he asked me how I was coming with my book on him. I told him that I was not making much progress because he preferred to talk about philosophy during our walks, while I wished he would talk more about his own life. He looked me in the eye and said, "No one is interested in my life; and, furthermore, my life is my work. If they are interested in me they can read my books." This was, to be certain, very discouraging for someone who has just begun the task of a biography. I did not press the issue any more that day but turned to Simone for help.

The next morning, Paul was in Paris, so Simone and I sat at the dining room table and she gave me the family history—who was born when, etc. She had a small notebook in which she kept a list of Paul's honorary doctorates, along with a few other items, including some of their friends' phone numbers.

That afternoon, Paul and I took another walk, this time in the opposite direction toward the Vallée aux Loups (Valley of the wolves) and sat on a terrace from which we had a magnificent view of the whole suburban area south of Paris, including a clear view of Orly Airport. On our walk, we passed the grove where the Nazis executed members of the French Resistance during the Occupation. It is now called "Martyrs of the Resistance." This led us back to the discussion of his military service. I asked him if, when the war broke out, he was prepared to kill someone. He said, "no"; but when I asked him if it was his pacifism which led to his reluctance, he replied, in a somewhat offended tone, "I am a patriot and I would have done what was required."

He then opened up a bit about his wartime experience, telling me his company of infantry had only a few machine guns and one cannon. They were behind the main French army at the Marne and their job was to gather up stragglers and deserters. He said that he was ordered to hold a bridge, which he did by blowing it up with a German tank on it. He laughed and said he got the Croix de Guerre with three palm leaves . . . , "but nobody is interested in these stories." The most moving experience he had, one which left a lasting impression, was when he and his captain were talking and a sniper shot the captain in the head. He was killed instantly, and Paul never forgot how fragile and contingent life is and how easy it could have been for the sniper to have chosen him. He later told me that what made this experience even worse is that it happened after they had been captured by the Germans. When they were surrounded and gave up, they had a sense of humiliation, but also a sense of relief that they would not be killed. The Germans made them cross the Marne and then marched them along the bank of the river. To make matters worse, Paul did not know whether it was a German sniper who fired or a French soldier mistaking them for Germans since they were walking with them.

After the bridge incident, they were sent, first on foot, later by train, to Pomerania in northern Germany to the POW camp for French officers. I have already told most of the Oflag experience, but not from conversations with Paul. He says he does not remember much of what happened, it was so monotonous, with one day, one month, one year blending into the next. When I found it remarkable that he couldn't remember more, he said, "When I left the camp, I closed the door behind me. No one is interested in those war stories. I refuse to be one of those veterans who make a life of retelling their stories."

A few days later, René Rémond accepted my request for an interview, which began in his office in Paris and continued while we walked to an appointment he had some distance away. He told me the story of Nanterre, just as he had told it in his book. He repeated several times that Ricoeur was an excellent administrator who had been betrayed my some of his friends and by the very faculty who had elected him. As to the rapidity with which the minister of the interior Marcellin sent in the police, Rémond thought it was a misunderstanding about how critical the situation was, while Ricoeur thinks that Marcellin tricked him or used him to show that Nanterre was out of control. In any case, Rémond thought that by resigning, it looked like Ricoeur was taking responsibility for what happened there between the police and the "enragés" and that Rémond got the credit for restoring normalcy to the university. Both of these impressions are incorrect, he said. He did say that the leftists tried to turn Ricoeur's youngest son, Etienne, who was a student in the lycée at the time, against his father.

When I returned to Chatenay, Paul was very interested in hearing what Rémond had to say. I repeated the conversation I had with him. Ricoeur agreed with Rémond, but added some details. He said that a professor of philosophy was storing molotov cocktails in his office for student use. A teacher in a lycée was fired because he led his students in the destruction of classrooms. He was appointed an assistant in the sociology department, a department completely dominated by the leftists. The minister of education found out about it and called Ricoeur, demanding to know if it was true and wanting an answer that same day. So, Ricoeur called the assistant in and told him he had no right to teach at Nanterre since he had been fired from his job at the lycée. (Because both were government jobs under the auspices of the minister of education, the assistant could not teach in the university after being fired from the other teaching job.) The assistant challenged him to call the police to have him removed, and he continued to "teach" there. What could Ricoeur do? The assistant would not have the right to give official grades, but other professors in the department would do it for him.

Paul said that the *Doyen* was powerless: He could not hire and fire; he could not protect the buildings and the personnel; and he had virtually no control over what department heads did. So he thought he did the right thing by resigning.

I had asked René Rémond why Ricoeur took the job in the first place. He told me that Ricoeur had written several articles advocating reform in the universities and that Ricoeur had a sense of responsibility for the collectivity, for the community. He chose to go to Nanterre with the hopes of making it into something more democratic, more humane than the Sorbonne. He saw his democratic ideals shattered by the fascists of the left and the fascists of the right, for whom imposing their particular vision of the world was much more important than any democratic ideal. Paul finished this conversation by saying, "Teaching in the United States saved my life, literally. I was terribly depressed after Nanterre. I have devoted my life to the university and teaching. So, it was important to me to go to Chicago and continue teaching after the terrible experience at Nanterre."

The next day, I was invited to lunch at the Ricoeurs. Olivier asked me how my interview with René Rémond went. Before I could say a word, Paul interjected that Rémond had said that the leftists had manipulated Etienne against him. Paul thought that was false, and Simone agreed. But Olivier said it was not altogether false since Etienne was living in a commune where there was an element of coercion.

Then Paul told the following story. One day one of the "enragés" (the angry, antisocial leftovers from the events of 1968) rode a draft horse into the hall that connects the buildings at Nanterre. The student had a stick with which he tried to "lance" Ricoeur. This was another of the long string of incidents that led up to the demonstrations in March of 1970 on the campus of the university at Nanterre. It turned out that the student lived in the same commune as Etienne. The commune members ejected this student as a thief and as a detriment to the commune. Ricoeur, who could not kick the student off the campus of the university, was accused by the leftists of being a "flic" (a cop), but it was the leftists who kicked the student out of their commune. Ricoeur asked, "Who were the flics?"

In the summer of 1982, I again visited Paul in Chatenay, where I stayed for six weeks. I lived in a small room on the top floor of the main building at Les Murs Blancs, above the apartment of Mme. Mounier. I ate frequently at the Ricoeurs and Paul and I continued our practice of long walks together. On one of our walks in the Parc de Sceaux, I asked him how he came to be associated with Emmanuel Mounier and the Esprit movement. He said that one of Mounier's friends was at the University of Rennes when Paul was a student there and that Mounier had visited the university. There was a "cercle Esprit" at Rennes and Paul was a member. He said that the first issue of *Esprit* came out in 1932, and the manifesto of a Christian, humanistic, socialism was just the thing he had been looking for. He was very active in the socialist party all during the 1930s and was at one time the secretary of the Young Socialists of Brittany.

Later in our conversation, I asked him his opinion about Roger Ikor's accusations against the French military professionals, especially about their unpreparedness for the war of 1940. Paul responded that, in large measure, it was the socialists who were to blame. "We were the pacifists," he said, "against the military and against any attempt to mobilize." He told me that he had more respect for some professional soldiers he knew in the POW camps than he did for the pacifists, in spite of his sympathy for pacifism. He recounted the story of one professional officer who, rather than eat the fat they were given in place of butter, used it to grease his boots, in spite of the very meager rations they had. Paul thought the professional officers suffered in the camps more than the teachers or others because of their sense of personal shame for being POWs.

When I told Paul I had read Ikor's book, his response was that he himself had very few memories of the camp. He had spent his time reading and writing philosophy and, later, after the formation of the "university," in giving courses. Ikor, on the other hand, was much more involved in clandestine political activities.

Since he had just retired from the University of Paris-Nanterre, I asked Paul who had been named to his chair. He said that he had recommended his friend and former student, Jacques Derrida, and that Derrida had applied but was not elected. He then nominated Michel Henry for the chair, but nothing happened.

Eventually, the minister of education eliminated the chair. This had become common in France, since there were fewer and fewer philosophy students.

I asked him why he had taught at the Institute of European Studies in the early 1960s. He said he thought it was to earn extra money; it was quite expensive to buy into Les Murs Blancs and he had a large family to support. He added that many French professors are interested in teaching American students because they are less blasé and less cynical and more eager to learn than French students. American students are not as well prepared as French students at the beginning of their university studies, but they are even with them at the end of the bachelor's degree. And, there is nothing in France that can compare to the thorough preparation of the American Ph.D. degree.

We also talked at length about *Time and Narrative*. Paul had given me a later version of Chapter 3 of Part I. I gave him a written critique which he took, along with one by his editor, François Wahl, to Préfailles a week later in order to give the draft of Part I a final going-over. My opinion was that he gave too much credit to others, especially the structuralists, and spent too much time carefully working through their positions before he gave his critique of them and then laid out his own position. He said he understood my criticism, but he owed a debt to those he had read, both contemporary and historical authors, and thought he should pay them and their work its just due. He said almost every philosopher has had a piece of the truth and none of them has had it all. He felt he should sort through their positions before he advanced his own.

In early June, Jean-Paul was in Paris and came out to Chatenay for dinner with Paul, Simone, and myself. Before dinner, the conversation was mostly about the "psychoanalytic scene" in France. Jean-Paul carefully reviewed the influence of Lacan and his effect on psychoanalysis in France. He added that most Lacanian psychoanalysts did not follow Lacan into the last theoretical stage inspired by his son-in-law, Jacques-Alain Miller. This was not so much because they thought the "mathemes" were wrong, but because they did not know what to do with them. They had no practical application in analysis. The whole history of Lacanism is one of splits, polemics, splinter groups, the formation and dissolution of associations, so his death did not change things very much. Most Lacanians do not recognize J.-A. Miller as a suitable successor, although they appreciate the work he and his group are doing to publish the seminars.

Paul waited patiently for his son to finish and then said that the problem is, anyone can say anything he wants. There is no careful argumentation, only invective and polemic. No one is held accountable for his statements. Paul contrasted this with the Anglo-American habits of careful philosophical argumentation, with its legalistic refutations, rejoinders, rebuttals, all focused on the philosophical claims themselves. Jean-Paul was unmoved by the comparison, probably be-cause he knew only the French style of theoretical exposition and argument.

The next week, I went by train with Paul and Simone to Nantes, where Paul picked up a rental car to use for the week. He told me how much he enjoyed driving, but that since they spent so much time in Chicago, where he did not drive, that he sometimes forgot exactly how to do it. That was evident during the forty-mile drive to Préfailles on narrow country roads. His shifting was sometimes erratic, and he was liable to go into the wrong gear. He was unflappa-ble and just said, "Excuse me," and tried again to find the correct gear.

Since we were the first to use the house at Préfailles for the summer, the neighbor had come over ahead of time to open the windows and air the house out. The cleaning lady had come by and put things in good order. Since there was no food in the house, we ate at the little hotel, near the beach. The next day, Paul and I shopped for groceries. He was welcomed back by everyone as an old friend, since he had spent his summers there since the late 1930s.

Later, Simone and I went through the family photographs, which were in small boxes scattered all over the house in different dressers or cabinets. Simone said she was very close to Alice, Paul's sister. It was her impression that Alice was neglected by Adèle and the grandparents, who showered their attention and affection on Paul. Simone said that Alice was especially courageous throughout her illness (tuberculosis), even to the end. One remarkable thing was that there were no pictures of Paul's mother, and the paternal grandparents never spoke about her. Paul and Simone knew few of the relatives on his mother's side of the family.

Simone told me what she knew about Paul's father, Jules. He was a professor of English at the lycée in Valence. He was mobilized in 1914 and reported missing in action in 1915. Several years later, his body was found with two others. Appar-ently he had been wounded by shrapnel, and while two of his comrades were dragging him back, another shell hit and buried all three of them.

The usual rhythm of a day at Préfailles was breakfast at 8:00 or 8:30, followed by shopping and reading. Simone would prepare the noon meal, frequently fea-turing grilled meat—at which Paul was the expert. He especially likes grilled lamb or steak and grilled fish. After a leisurly meal and coffee, Paul and I would take a two- or three-hour walk along the "Côte sauvage," the rocky shoreline along that part of the coast of Brittany. We would usually stop for something to drink at a café. Paul generally drank tea, while I would have a beer.

After our return to the house, we would read the newspaper and then watch the 8:00 P.M. news on the television. Then we would have a light supper of sau-sages, cheese, soup, leftovers from the noon meal, and bread. The discussions at the dinner table were about current events in France, or about trouble spots in other parts of the world. During this summer, the British-Argentine war of the Falkland Islands was being fought, and it was a frequent topic. Everyone went to bed about 10:00 P.M. It was a very relaxing, very enjoyable experience.

On our walks, we discussed issues in philosophy, or the recent books of French or American authors. I recall a long discussion of Jacques Derrida. Paul said that the problem he found with Derrida's work is that it is hard to follow and there are very few arguments. He said many French authors thought it was enough to simply assert something. They tended to ignore the arguments of other philosophers, except for Heidegger and a very few others, and they do not give arguments in support of their positions. This was the same criticism he made of Lacan at the dinner with Jean-Paul. Derrida had been discovered by American universities and he was lecturing there extensively. But he was the darling of the literature departments, while the philosophy departments were still not familiar with his work. American philosophers tended to be put off by his style.

One afternoon, a large delivery truck came up in front of the house and the driver came to the door. Paul was very excited, because his "serre" or greenhouse was being delivered. The driver was directed to drive around the block and through the alley to the back gate of the garden. I helped the driver unload about six large, and very heavy, boxes. The greenhouse was in kit form, with aluminum framing, and many boxes of glass panes for the sides and top. It was about 9′ by 12′ and designed in the Netherlands to be assembled on-site. I told Paul I would assemble it for him, and so I pored over the directions. They were quite straightforward; however, the sack of bolts, nuts, and other fasteners was missing. Paul called the large Parisian department store where he bought it, and they promised to send a replacement kit of fasteners in a week or two. It was Paul's son Marc who finally assembled the greenhouse later that summer.

Having a small greenhouse in the garden is not uncommon in Europe but Paul's use of it was. When the weather was nice at Préfailles, the grandchildren always played outside or went to the beach. However, when it was cold or rainy, the grandchildren played in the house. In this case, Paul could not find a quiet corner in which to read, reflect, and write his philosophical articles. So the greenhouse was—and is—Paul's private retreat. He has a simple table, chair, and small bookcase which holds the twenty or so books most relevant to the topic he is working on at the moment. The top of the greenhouse is covered with bamboo mats and is shaded by vines and trees. The sliding door, along with some of the opening windows, gives sufficient ventilation. I thought it was an ingenious way to solve the problem of combining intellectual work with the joy of having his grandchildren around during the summer.

After our return to Chatenay, we took several more walks. I prepared a list of questions I wanted to ask Paul in an interview in English which I wanted to use in my course on hermeneutics the following fall semester. One afternoon, we went over the questions, and we began taping the interview the next morning. Part way through, Paul had to go to Paris, and so we finished it later that day. This was the first of the formal interviews that are published for the first time in this book.

In June 1983, there was an international conference in Paris at the Sorbonne devoted to Ricoeur. A large international audience heard scholars from many countries give papers on various aspects of Ricoeur's work. There were about thirty presentations over a five-day period. Paul and Simone were there for all of them, and then hosted a reception at their house in Chatenay for all of the participants. The papers were given in the ornate Louis Liard lecture hall, in the Sorbonne, just off the courtyard. It was a moving moment for many of us who were Paul's students, to speak from the podium in that room while Paul was in the audience. It was a reversal of the experience we had as students listening to Paul make the presentations.

In May of 1984, my wife and I flew to Raleigh, North Carolina, to visit the Ricoeurs. They were spending one of their three periods at the National Center for the Humanities, in Research Triangle Park. Scholars are invited to spend from several months to a year at the center working on their books and articles. Each scholar has a private office and they take a noon meal in common. The visiting scholars take turns reading papers about their work and soliciting the ideas and comments of the others at the center.

During this spring semester, the Ricoeurs had rented a large house from a professor on sabbatical leave. Their friends the Lacocques also took a leave and came to North Carolina with the Ricoeurs. They shared the house, and André and Paul worked together at the humanities center. Paul picked us up at the Raleigh airport; he was driving André's new car with electric windows and locks. When we got to the parking-lot toll booth, Paul could not get the window to go down, and, as he pushed the row of electric buttons on the door, matters just got worse. He locked the windows, so even the window button wouldn't work, and he locked the doors, so he couldn't open the door to pay the toll. Finally, when a long line had formed behind us, Paul said "Sorry" to the attendant and we drove off. Paul had a great sense of humor about the incident and we laughed about the unintended results of high technology.

The next day the six of us loaded into André's car and toured the area. Paul was especially interested in the local pottery industry, still based on individual artisans working in their homes or attached shops. They had developed over the years a very attractive and unique style. Paul and Simone bought a number of pieces both out of a sense of artistic appreciation and a sense of admiration for the artisans themselves. I think they were also touched by the similarity of those artisans with their son Etienne, who is a silversmith in the Pyrenees in southern France.

Later during that visit we went to Duke University and also walked the campus of the University of North Carolina. Paul talked about his great appreciation for American universities and his utter amazement at the wealth of the private universities such as Duke and his own university, Chicago. I was especially pleased that this visit gave my wife, Sharon, and Simone a chance to renew their friendship.

In April of 1986, I went to Chicago to see Paul and Simone. This was the second time I had visited them there. A few days before going, I received an unexpected phone call from Michel Winock, the French historian whom I met when we lived in the Ricoeurs' house for the first time in 1974. He and his family lived on the third floor and their children were playmates of my son. Michel informed me of Olivier's suicide. His call was timely; otherwise, I would have gone to Chicago unaware, and Paul would have had to tell me.

Paul and Simone were staying with their friends, André and Claire Lacocque. When I arrived, Paul was the only one home. It was a very tearful and emotional greeting, since it was only a month since Olivier's death. A little later, Paul told me of the double shock of his friend Mircea Eliade's death two weeks before, only a few days after Paul and Simone had arrived in Chicago. They had had dinner with the Eliades just two nights before they received Christinel's call that Mircea was gravely ill. The loss of one of their best friends, added to the loss of their son, devastated Paul and Simone. Since Olivier was one of my dear friends, too, the three days in Chicago were much like a funeral all over again for us.

In my Introduction to this book, I announced my intention to write very little about the Ricoeur children, both to respect their privacy and because, for the most part, I can tell the story of Paul and Simone without telling theirs. The exception is Olivier. I feel obliged to write about him because Paul dedicated *From Text to Action* to him and he has an "Interlude" on Tragic Action dedicated to Olivier in *Oneself as Another*. Also, after Olivier's death, Paul began to add "suffering" to the phrase "human action" whenever he wrote about his existential theme of human action and suffering.

I have already mentioned the conversations Olivier and I had during the fall of 1974. Olivier was very friendly, personable, and handsome. He was always helpful and, most of the time, joyful. But Olivier had some severe problems as well. He was homosexual, alcoholic, and, at times, a drug user. His drug of choice was ether, and when he sniffed it he became morose and suicidal. On one occasion that I remember vividly, he was using ether. The odors were coming up into the apartment and I asked him to stop. He came upstairs and told my wife that he was thinking of suicide. While she talked to him and comforted him, I called his brother, Marc. Marc told me that this was not the first time Olivier had mentioned suicide, but that he got over it fairly quickly and that we should not be overly concerned. In an hour or so, Olivier was in better spirits and he returned to his apartment below the Ricoeurs'.

Olivier had gone to a filmmaking school in Paris for several years and was very knowledgeable about the production end of filmmaking. He worked as an assistant producer. When he was working, he was generally much better, though he had his lapses into alcohol and drugs then as well. Olivier also worked as a typist for Paul. Especially when Paul was in Chicago, he would send Olivier tapes on which he had dictated the French version of his articles and papers. Olivier would send back the typed version and Paul would make his corrections on it. Olivier had done this on the Gifford Lectures, shortly before his death.

There are many twists and turns to Olivier's story which I choose not to retell here. Most of his life was an unending battle with his personal demons. What is unknown, however, is why Olivier chose the day he did and the manner in which he committed suicide. He was living on the top floor of an apartment building on rue du Temple in Paris. He used a ladder to climb on the roof, and then jumped to the street below. Paul was in Prague and returned immediately. Olivier's funeral was two days later.

During our grief in Chicago, Paul told me more than once that somehow the most difficult children are the ones whom parents love the most. I certainly know the pain Olivier caused Paul and Simone—and his close friends—as well as the enormous love all of us had for Olivier.

In the spring of 1987, I returned briefly to Chatenay where I had dinner with the Ricoeurs, and a few days later we spent several hours together at the end of an afternoon. At dinner, we discussed Paul's recently published collection, *From Text to Action*. He said it had been reviewed favorably, although the French readers were still puzzled by his frequent references to Anglo-American philosophers such as John Rawls, H. L. A. Hart, and Anthony Kenny, to mention only three. The goal of this book is to bridge the gap in Paul's publications in France between *The Rule of Metaphor* and *Time and Narrative*. His hermeneutics is quite out of joint with the writings of Derrida, Foucault, Lacan, and others who dominated the French literary and intellectual scene during this period. Paul said that it was his job to write books on the questions which intrigued him, and it was the job of others to criticize and judge them.

In the summer of 1988, I returned again to Chatenay, with David and Audrey Stewart of Ohio University. We had a small grant to photocopy some of Ricoeur's unpublished manuscripts to put in an archive at Ohio University for the use of scholars. We were able to copy some 1,500 pages during the week. A bit of misfortune for the Ricoeurs became a stroke of luck for us. Over the Easter holiday that spring, burglars broke into the Ricoeurs' home. They scattered the contents of drawers and cabinets all over the rooms. In particular, all of the books were thrown on the floor. (This is the result of the French habit—or the myth of the French habit—of stashing currency in books.) When the books and papers were put back, they were put in an order that did not exist before. As a consequence, I found Paul's POW camp journals, which I had not seen before even though I had lived in the house on several occasions.

These journals are very interesting on several counts. First, unlike many journals, they say not one word about daily life in the camp. There is not one line about wishing to be back in France, to see his wife and young children, of freedom, of food, of warmth—all things lacking in the camp. There were no political tracts condemning war, or governments, or weak armies, or ruthless armies. Second, the journals are several drafts of parts of what later became *Freedom and Nature*. Paul worked and reworked several themes. Third, parts of the journals are his understanding and reflection on the texts he was reading, especially Jaspers and later Husserl. Paul passed his five years as a POW not unlike the five years in the early 1930s when he was a student. Most of his time was spent reading, reflecting, and writing. Roger Ikor writes of Ricoeur as always having an aline ink on his fingers and face from the leaky pens they used and Paul's habit of rubbing his forehead or nose when he was concentrating especially hard.

After a week of photocopying manuscripts, David and Audrey Stewart departed for a vacation in Greece, and I went to Cérisy-la-Salle, a chateau in Normandy used as a conference center, for the "Décade de Paul Ricoeur." This was an international conference held in honor of Ricoeur. There were about one hundred people in attendance, with some twenty-three invited papers. The participants arrived for a dinner and introductions on August 1, 1988, and the conference was opened the next morning by Jean Greisch, dean of the Faculty of Philosophy of the Institut Catholique in Paris. The first paper was given by Michel Henry, professor emeritus of the University Paul-Valéry at Montpellier.

The daily rhythm of the conference began with breakfast at 8:00 A.M. taken, as were all the meals, in common in the two large dining halls of the chateau. The first paper would be given at 9:00 A.M. in the chateau's ornate library, whose walls were lined with bookcases with wire-mesh doors. The speaker would give his or her paper and then there would be a coffee break of twenty to thirty minutes. At about 11:00 the session would reconvene with either more presentations or with continued discussion of the previous paper. It was especially satisfying for the participants to have long discussion periods during which everyone who wanted to join in had a chance to offer comments or ask questions of the speaker. Paul had something to say about every paper and was, as is his custom, extremely gracious with each speaker, even when he differed sharply from the speaker's thesis or claims.

After an excellent Norman meal, everyone would assemble outside, in front of the chateau, where there were tables and chairs set up for coffee. The afternoon session began at 3:00 and continued until 4:30 or 5:00. Between the last session and dinner at 7:30, people walked in the extensive gardens of the chateau, read, rested, or met for conversation in any of the many rooms of the chateau. After dinner there was music and conversation available in the attic-room, outfitted with a grand piano, and in the basement game room.

Paul and Simone attended every session and took their meals in the dining rooms, always trying to sit with different people so that, over the course of the ten days, they could meet everyone who attended. At coffee and after the sessions, Paul was always available for conversation, whether it was with one of his university colleagues, a foreign colleague who had written books and articles on his work, or a graduate student doing a thesis on his work.

On August 11, Paul gave the final paper. He began with a tribute to the organizers, Jean Greisch and Richard Kearney (the latter a professor of philosophy at University College, Dublin), and to all those who presented papers. His presentation, "L'Attestation: Entre phénoménologie et ontologie," ("Attestation: Between Phenomenology and Ontology"), was a long working paper preparing the way for the last chapter of *Oneself as Another*. He took up two of the principal concepts in that book, "*ipséité*" (self-sameness) and "*attestation*" (a level of truth claim between the certainty of Descartes' *cogito* and Nietzsche's *illusion*. Both of these concepts are new approaches to old philosophical problems which Ricoeur introduces for the first time in *Oneself as Another*. The discussion afterwards was animated. Later, the lunch was a kind of celebration of an extraordinarily successful conference.

In May of 1990, I went to Chicago and interviewed Paul, for the third of the four interviews published in this book. I asked him about his impressions of Cérisy-la-Salle. He said,

> The condition I had put to them [Greisch and Kearney] to take part in this *Décade* was that it would not be about me, but about the problems with which I struggled. This is why, among the 15 or 20 essays which were read, only one fourth may be said to be about me or a presentation of my work. So it is more a confrontation of different points of view concerning the main problems which I covered during these thirty or forty years, precisely, language, psychoanalysis, and literature and metaphorical language, and all their related problems. And, I must say that this was for me a very rewarding experience because we spent ten days together without anybody leaving. So, we became acquainted and there was a kind of common

language and nobody was aggressive and nobody wanted to embarrass me, but at the same time there was no subservient attitude. (See p. 117–118 below)

Other people, like Jean Greisch, told me the same thing. Since this was the first and only conference at Cérisy-la-Salle I attended, I did not know exactly what they were comparing it to. Later, I was told that some of these "décades" have become shouting matches, with rival factions (or "chapels" as the French call these groups of followers) and people leaving the conference in a huff. Sometimes the speaker tries to embarrass the guest of honor to whose work the conference is dedicated. Or, one group tries to embarrass a speaker who is not a member of the inside group, and so forth. I thought the conference reflected Paul's own ethic and attitudes and that his principles of giving the other's words the most generous interpretation possible, respect for those with whom you disagree, acknowledgment of the contributions of others, cordiality in personal relations, and civility in argument, were practiced by the participants and the audience.

In 1980, I had asked Paul why his replies to his critics were so gentle, when sometimes the critics were so polemical. Why didn't he ever punch back? He gave me two answers: First, he said you cannot teach someone when you are hitting them. Second, he showed me his response to J.-P. Valabréga's review of *Freud and Philosophy,* in which Valabréga insinuates and implies and obliquely accuses Ricoeur of plagiarism of Lacan's ideas. In the next issue of *Critique,* the journal in which Valabréga's review was published, Ricoeur's letter of response was published. Paul answers Valabréga's claims point-for-point and does so with a very direct and powerful language appropriate to a defense. He says he does not ordinarily answer critics, but Valabréga had attacked not only his book but his intellectual honesty. This was intolerable.

In late June of 1991, I again visited Paul in Chatenay. When I got there, Paul had lunch prepared and told me that Simone was in the hospital. She had a circulation problem in her carotid artery and they were doing tests to determine the most appropriate treatment. Simone had already arranged with Anne Mounier, the daughter of Emmanuel and Paulette Mounier, to have her late mother's apartment at Les Murs Blancs for me to use during my stay. Paulette had died just a few months previously. Her optimism, her smiling face, and her indomitable spirit are sorely missed by everyone who knew her. Simone, in particular, felt this loss since they were such good friends and constant companions.

During the next week and a half, Paul visited Simone daily while they waited for the diagnosis and recommended treatment for Simone's condition. During the last week in June, Antenne 2, one of the national television networks in France, filmed daily for an hour-long program on Ricoeur. Olivier Abel, a good friend of Paul's and a professor at the Institut Protestant in Paris, did the interviewing. The interviews were filmed in the living room of Ricoeur's house, in the garden, at Nanterre, at the Sorbonne, and at the Orangerie in the Tuileries Garden. It took about five days of filming to make the special one-hour program.

Our conversations during this week were mostly about current political problems on the international level and in France and the U.S. Paul had been engaged in writing articles on the concept of justice and its application to particular economies. At one point, he asked me if I knew that he had been awarded the philosophy prize, worth 50,000 francs ($10,000) from the Academie Française. After receiving the Hegel Prize in Germany, and many honorary doctorates from universities around the world, this was a very important honor from his own country. The television program on him and this prize, along with the constant interviews in magazines and newspapers, signaled his "rediscovery" in his native country.

The next day I went with Paul to Nanterre where that day's filming would take place. It was set up in one of the large lecture halls. The director had written in big letters on the blackboard, "Ricoeur, vieux clown" (Ricoeur, old fool), a slogan that had been painted on the wall of the central corridor linking several classroom buildings together. Paul patiently recounted for Olivier Abel and the film crew the events leading up to the disturbances in 1968 and the later ones in 1970. He told us that one day in the spring of 1968, Daniel Cohn-Bendit stood up in the middle of one of his lectures and said, "It's over for you, Ricoeur," at which point every student got up in unison and left the room. He said it was a lesson in the power of the word.

In 1968 Cohn-Bendit took his student revolution to the Sorbonne and left Nanterre in relative peace. However, in 1969 and 1970, the campus was infected with the "enragés" (angry ones) who had no political program and just wanted to smash and wreck things. During the events of 1968, the students had a political program of remaking society. Paul was divided between their social idealism— a version of which he shared with them—and his philosophical conviction that the university is one of the most important social institutions. In fact, the university is the one institution which has as a charge to critique other institutions and to propose how they should be changed.

At breakfast the next day, we talked about Bennington and Derrida's biography/autobiography of Derrida. Paul showed me his copy of the book, which was signed by both of them. He said he found Bennington's text elegant and very well-written. As for Derrida, he thought it was vain to center his autobiographical discussion on his circumcision. I was surprised to learn that in 1962 Derrida was Ricoeur's assistant at the Sorbonne. In the book it says that when Derrida was a candidate for Ricoeur's chair at Nanterre after Ricoeur's retirement, the minister of education, Alice Saunier-Seité, had abolished the chair.

After a week's absence from Paris, I returned to Chatenay and the next day had breakfast with Paul and Simone. They talked of the "limbo" they were in. The tests on Simone were inconclusive and Paul said they had to choose between "the worst case and the worst case." He worried that if they did nothing, she would have another stroke; but there were grave dangers in any intervention, whether surgical or medical. Paul wanted to go to Préfailles for July and August, but the nearest medical facility was at Nantes, some 50 kilometers away. After waiting two weeks for Simone's condition to stabilize, they did go to Préfailles for the rest of the summer.

Once Simone was home from the hospital, Paul could finally get to his correspondence. He showed me a pile of letters about two feet high on a chair in his study. He dictated his responses and gave the tape to a secretary he had hired to type his letters. She then returned them to him for his signature. After breakfast, we went into Paul's study and began taping the last of the four interviews which are published in this book.

A few days later, I had lunch with Elisabeth Roudinesco. She told me she was writing a biography of Jacques Lacan, as a follow-up to her two-volume history of the psychoanalytic movement in France. We had an animated and long conversation about the intellectual scene in France. She told me that Ricoeur had become famous again in France. She thought this was because people had become weary with the frenzy of political action, overly dramatic conflicts, and abstract theorizing. Intellectuals of her age were taking flight to history, history of philosophy, literature—rather than to literary theory—and an interest in religion had reappeared. She said she had gone to the university in the late 1960s and did not know of Ricoeur then.

We had a long discussion about the Lacanian movement. At the end of our lunch, she asked me if Ricoeur had any letters from Lacan or any photographs of the two of them. I told her that I had never seen any letters from Lacan or photos of him with Ricoeur, but that I would ask Paul.

The next day, I had lunch with Paul, Simone, and their daughter, Noëlle, who had come from Marseilles to visit her parents. After a long discussion about Lacan and other topics, I asked Paul if he had any letters or photos of himself and Lacan. He said he never saved any letters and, in any case, Lacan had never written him one. As for photos, he said he did not know, but he did not think so.

We spoke at some length about the problem Elisabeth Roudinesco would have in writing a biography of Lacan since the Lacan archives are under the control of Jacques-Alain Miller, Lacan's son-in-law. She does not have access to those materials. I said that, as a historian, she was at a disadvantage without access to primary sources. Paul said that he could not take Lacan's published seminars seriously as long as the original tapes are not public. Then he returned to the paper he gave at Bonneval on the unconscious. After he delivered the paper, Lacan had praised it and congratulated him, and even gave him a ride back to Paris. But when the proceedings were published, the part of the discussion where Lacan praised his paper was omitted. Paul called the editor to find out why and was told that Lacan had edited it out. What had happened between Bonneval and the publication of the proceedings was the famous incident in Rome.

After lunch, we went to the living room for coffee. I showed Paul the book I was given the previous day at Nanterre, when I went to the office of the president (formerly the office of the *doyen*) to take some pictures. The president, Paul Larivaille, told me the campus and the office were completely different than they had been when Ricoeur was there. He gave me the book celebrating the twenty-fifth anniversary of the University of Paris-Nanterre. Paul was fascinated by some of the pictures in the book from the 1968–70 period, especially the photograph of the "student" on horseback on the campus and in the library. He reiterated the story of how this student tried to lance him in the corridor, and then tried to trap him between the horse and the wall. He followed up with the story of this student being expelled from his son Etienne's commune. Paul remarked that the leftists expelled the student from their commune, but he was not permitted to expel him from the university.

In response to my question about the pictures of Paul and Lacan, Noëlle and Simone got out several boxes of photographs. Except for the pictures of their fiftieth wedding anniversary in 1985, almost all of the pictures in their boxes were taken by others and given to them. Paul and Simone simply did not carry a camera and take pictures. Paul never kept a diary. Later, he showed me a box of his old agendas. I thought I had found a treasure trove of sources for my biographical essay. Rather, there were no important things—such as the Gifford Lectures—written in the agendas. I asked Paul about it. He said he could remember the important things, so he only wrote down in the agendas the appointments or things he thought he might forget. Thus, the only entries are the most mundane, appointments with students, meetings with colleagues, and so forth.

In the course of looking at the pictures, we came across one where Paul is receiving an honorary doctorate from the University of Tilburg. He is carrying an absurd-looking long leather box which contained the diploma, hand-lettered in Latin on parchment. Simone got the box out and we looked at the diploma. Rolled up with the it was another certificate which turned out to be a posthumous award of the Croix de Guerre for Paul's father, Jules, "Mort pour la France, Septembre 26, 1915." Paul asked Simone why it was in that box. Simone said she simply wanted to find a safe place to store it. When she was rolling up the diploma and the certificate, Paul told her not to put his father's certificate in with his diploma, since he felt that his father's award was so much more important than his own. He said, "You do not store a fine napkin in with the dish rags." Simone found another cardboard tube for the certificate.

I told Paul that for someone so interested in history, in time, in traces, he had left very few. He said, once again, "my works are my traces. The history of my philosophical views may be interesting, but the history of my life is 'nulle' [nothing]."

In the summers of 1992 and 1993, I returned to France and visited the Ricoeurs in Préfailles, for three or four days each time. These visits were much like the previous ones, with long walks along the rocky coast, stops at a café for tea or beer, discussions of current events and of various philosophers whom Paul had just read. In 1993, I showed Paul the first thirty pages of my biographical essay. This provoked a discussion about the facts surrounding his mother's death. There was a great deal of uncertainty, and Paul and Simone had differing opinions about whether she died during or just after Paul's birth, or sometime later from other causes. The family Bible settled the issue with the date of his mother's death in September of 1913. We also talked more about their childhoods in Rennes.

Paul repeated what he has told me many times: "No one is interested in my life; and besides, my life is my work. If you want to write about me, just write about my philosophical books and articles." I believe he is mistaken, but the real test is in the hands of the reader.

· 3 ·

PHILOSOPHICAL ESSAY
PERSONAL IDENTITY

D URING THE DECADE of the 1980s, Paul Ricoeur published five major
works: three volumes of *Time and Narrative*;[1] *From Text to Action*,[2] an
edited version of many of his articles published in English during the
late 1970s and early 1980s; and, most recently, *Oneself as Another*.[3] In 1980, at the
beginning of this prolific period, Ricoeur had already retired from the University
of Paris-Nanterre and was thinking of reducing his teaching at the University of
Chicago. Several years later, he was named the John Nuveen Professor Emeritus
at the University of Chicago and limited his teaching there to one quarter per
year. He was then sixty-seven years old, and, after an extraordinary intellectual
career, was widely known and highly regarded both in France and in the United
States. He had clearly earned his retirement.

But, retirement is not his style. Rather, he began a new intellectual journey
which expanded beyond the hermeneutics he practiced in the 1970s to an understanding of the philosophical power of narratives. His three-volume work, *Time
and Narrative*, excited a renewed interest in his philosophy after a ten-year self-
imposed exile from the French university scene. During this period Ricoeur
lived, worked, lectured, and published primarily *outside* of France. Thus, in the
mid–1980s, his French readers needed to "catch up" with the work he had been
doing since the last major work he had published in France, *La métaphore vive*.[4]
The articles which are in edited and abridged form in the collection *Du texte à
l'action* were, with a few exceptions, either written and published in English, or
they were written in French but published outside of France.

---

* An earlier version of this chapter was published as "The Self as Another," in *Philosophy Today*
37, no. 1 (Spring 1993).

1. Paul Ricoeur, *Time and Narrative*, vols. 1, 2, 3, trans. K. Blamey and D. Pellauer (Chicago:
University of Chicago Press, 1984, 1985, 1988 respectively). Translation of *Temps et Récit* Tomes
I, II, III (Paris: Le Seuil, 1983, 1984, 1985 respectively).

2. Paul Ricoeur, *From Text to Action: Essays in Hermeneutics II*, trans. Kathleen Blamey and
John B. Thompson (Evanston: Northwestern University Press, 1991). Translation of *Du Texte à
l'action, Essais d'herméneutique II* (Paris: Le Seuil, 1986).

3. Paul Ricoeur, *Oneself As Another*, trans. Kathleen Blamey (Chicago: University of Chicago
Press, 1992). Translation of *Soi-Même Comme Un Autre* (Paris: Le Seuil, 1990). Numbers in parentheses refer to page numbers in *Oneself As Another*.

4. Paul Ricoeur, *La métaphore vive* (Paris: Le Seuil, 1974). Translated as *The Rule of Metaphor:
Multi-Disciplinary Studies of the Creation of Meaning in Language*, trans. R. Czerny with K. Mc-
Laughlin and J. Costello (Toronto: University of Toronto Press, 1977).

After finishing the third volume of *Time and Narrative*, Ricoeur began work on the Gifford Lectures, which he gave in Edinburgh in the winter of 1986. The lectures were written in French and an abridged English version was actually read. Ricoeur then revised the first version by expanding several chapters. The second edition follows closely the order and topics of the first edition. This version was first given as lectures at the University of Munich in the same year. Yet Ricoeur was not satisfied with his text and continued for two more years to work and rework it. This was time well spent: *Oneself as Another* is, in my opinion, Ricoeur's most elegantly written, clearly organized, and closely argued work. This is high praise for an author whose work as a whole exemplifies these traits.

What I intend to do here is to give a synopsis of the book in order to show what the question of personal identity is and how Ricoeur progressively argues for a concept of personal identity that is inextricably bound up with a concept of the other and the relation between the self and the other. Then, I will give a more detailed account of the three chapters on ethics. These chapters are interesting in their own right, and they come as close as anything Ricoeur has written to being a clear account of his "philosophical ethics." He has written many articles on individual moral or political concepts and concerns, but he has never written a theoretical work on ethics. These chapters serve as his "groundwork for a metaphysics of morals."

My second goal in this essay is to point out some of the things we, his students, learned about philosophy from Paul Ricoeur, as well as to comment on some of the constant features in his philosophical style. Above all, Paul Ricoeur is a *teacher* of philosophy. He taught us to do a careful reading of philosophical texts, to always give the most generous interpretation to ambiguous or obscure texts, and to give full credit to those we have read and from whom we have learned. His fundamental thesis as a philosopher is that virtually every philosopher, ancient, modern, or contemporary, has seen a piece of the truth. Now our task is to adjudicate among competing interpretations, each of which claims to be absolute.

The title itself of this book, *Oneself as Another*, indicates the three converging themes which make up this work: a reflexive meditation on the self or subject; a dialectic on the meaning of the word "*même*" or "same" in the sense of identical (*idem*) or in the sense of "one and the same" (*ipse*), or selfhood; a dialectic between the self and the "other." Ricoeur's meditation takes place within the context of the history of the philosophy of the subject and, in particular, of the philosophy of Descartes and Nietzsche. For Descartes, the *Cogito* is both indubitable and the ultimate foundation of all that can be known. For Nietzsche, on the contrary, the *Cogito* is the name of an illusion. Ricoeur, in his typically dialectic mode, says, "the hermeneutics of the self is placed at an equal distance from the apology of the *cogito* and from its overthrow"(4).

One of the most important dialectics in Ricoeur's philosophy is between the auto-foundational claims of idealistic philosophies of the self, such as Descartes' and Husserl's, and the skeptical philosophies of the "masters of suspicion," Nietzsche, Marx, and Freud. The reflective and hermeneutic philosophy Ricoeur practices is the contrary of a philosophy of the immediate. This is why Ricoeur, the French translator of Husserl's *Ideen I,* rejected from the beginning both the transcendental *epoché* and the idealist version of Husserl's phenomenology. Ricoeur says, "The first truth—*I am, I think*—remains as abstract and empty as it is invincible; it has to be 'mediated' by the ideas, actions, works, institutions, and monuments that objectify it."[5] Thus, Ricoeur rejects the classical picture of consciousness as a veridical "mirror of nature" and says we gain self-knowledge through the long route of the interpretations of texts, monuments, and cultural forms.

Ricoeur's goal is to develop a hermeneutic of the self that bridges the gap between the *cogito* and the anti-*cogito.* He asks, "To what extent can one say that the hermeneutics of the self developed here occupies an epistemological (and ontological, as I shall state in the tenth study) place, situated beyond the alternative of the *cogito* and the anti-*cogito?*"(16).

In his preface, Ricoeur sets forth three conceptual themes which guide his study of the self: the use of "self" in natural languages, "same" in the sense of *idem* and *ipse,* and the correlation between the self and the other-than-self. "To these three grammatical features correspond the three major features of the hermeneutics of the self, namely, the detour of reflection by way of analysis, the dialectic of selfhood and sameness, and finally the dialectic of selfhood and otherness"(16). The whole hermeneutic is led by the question, *who:* who speaks? who acts? who tells a story? and who is the subject of moral imputation?

The first grouping (chapters 1 and 2) is based on a *philosophy of language* both as semantics and as pragmatics. This analytic stage is made necessary by the indirect status of the self. Hermeneutics is always a philosophy of detour; the hermeneutics of the self must take a detour through the analysis of the language in which we talk about the self.

The second group (chapters 3 and 4) is based on a *philosophy of action* in the sense this has taken in analytic philosophy. The interest here is in language about action and in speech acts where the agent of an action designates himself as the one who acts. "The questions '*Who is speaking?*' and '*Who is acting?*' appear in this way to be closely interconnected"(17). Ricoeur reminds us that these long analytic forays are "characteristic of the indirect style of a hermeneutics of the

---

5. Paul Ricoeur, *Freud and Philosophy,* trans. Dennis Savage (New Haven: Yale University Press, 1970): 43.

self, in stark contrast to the demand for immediacy belonging to the cogito"(17).

The third grouping (chapters 5 and 6) is centered on the question of *personal identity*. This is the place of the dialectic between identity (*idem*)and identity (*ipse*) which arises from the second grammatical trait of *soi-même* (oneself) and the ambiguity of the word *même* (same). Here Ricoeur links narrative identity with the philosophy of action, since narrative is the "imitation of action" (*mimesis*). "At the same time, and correlatively, the subject of the action recounted will begin to correspond to the broader concept of the *acting and suffering* individual, which our analytic-hermeneutical procedure is capable of eliciting"(18).

The fourth group (chapters 7, 8, and 9) makes a final detour through the ethical and moral determinations of action. "It is in the three ethical studies that the dialectic of the *same* and the *other* will find its appropriate philosophical development"(18). Ricoeur admits that his studies appear to be fragmentary and lack a unity. He says, "The fragmentary character of these studies results from the analytic-reflective structure that imposes arduous detours on our hermeneutics, beginning as early as the first study"(19). The thematic unity is found in *human action*. But human action does not serve as an ultimate foundation of some set of derived disciplines. Rather, there is an analogical unity because of the polysemy of "action" and because of "the variety and contingency of the questions that activate the analyses leading back to the reflection on the self"(19–20).

The thread which unifies Ricoeur's analyses is *description, narration, prescription*. Narrative identity serves "a transitional and relational function between the description that prevails in the analytical philosophies of action and the prescription that designates all the determinations of action by means of a generic term on the basis of the predicates 'good' and 'obligatory'"(20).

The final study (chapter 10) explores the ontological consequences of the hermeneutics of the self. Ricoeur claims that the dialectic between the "same" and the "other" will prevent an ontology of act and power from becoming encased in a tautology. "The polysemy of otherness, which I shall propose in the tenth study, will imprint upon the entire ontology of acting the seal of the diversity of sense that foils the ambition of arriving at an ultimate foundation, characteristic of the cogito philosophies"(21).

Another characteristic which distinguishes Ricoeur's hermeneutics of the self from the philosophies of the *cogito* is the type of certainty appropriate to the hermeneutics, in contradistinction to the claims of self-evidence and self-foundation of the philosophies of the *cogito*. Ricoeur uses the word "attestation" to describe the level of certitude appropriate to his hermeneutics. With respect to the "epistemological exaltation" of Descartes' *cogito* and its destruction by Nietzsche and his followers, Ricoeur claims, "Attestation may appear to require less than the one and more than the other."(21) It is opposed to the kind of certainty claims of *épistemé*, of science, "taken in the sense of ultimate and self-founding knowledge"(21). Attestation is a kind of *belief*, not in the doxic sense of "I believe that . . . " but in the sense of "I believe in. . . ." Since attestation is a much weaker claim than the foundational claims of the *cogito*, it is always vulnerable. "This vulnerability will be expressed in the permanent threat of suspicion, if we allow that suspicion is the specific contrary of attestation. The kinship between attestation and testimony is verified here: there is no 'true' testimony without 'false' testimony. But there is no recourse against false testimony than another that is more credible; and there is no recourse against suspicion but a more reliable attestation"(22). Another way Ricoeur defines attestation is as "the *assurance of being oneself acting and suffering*. This assurance remains the ultimate recourse against all suspicion"(22). He finishes laying out his thesis and his plan of study by saying, "As credence without any guarantee, but also as trust greater than any suspicion, the hermeneutics of the self can claim to hold itself at an equal distance from the cogito exalted by Descartes and from the cogito that Nietzsche proclaimed forfeit. The reader will judge whether the investigations that follow live up to this claim"(23).

The notion of "attestation" is a middle ground between apodictic certainty—which is only rarely attainable—and perpetual suspicion, and it is, he says, the level of certainty appropriate to hermeneutics. In his influential article "The Model of the Text,"[6] Ricoeur uses the analogy with judicial reasoning and discourse to show the kind of certainty appropriate to hermeneutical interpretations in literary criticism and in the social sciences. The key is the polemical character of validation. Ricoeur says,

> In front of the court, the plurivocity common to texts and to actions is exhibited in the form of a conflict of interpretations, and the final interpretation appears as a verdict to which it is possible to make appeal. Like legal utterances, all interpretations in the field of literary criticism and in the social sciences may be challenged, and the question 'what can defeat a claim' is common to all argumentative situations. Only in the tribunal is there a moment when the procedures of appeal are exhausted. But it is because the decision of the judge is implemented by the force of public power. Neither in literary criticism, nor in the social sciences, is there such a last word. Or if there is any, we call that violence.[7]

In juridical arguments, we recognize levels of certainty appropriate to different situations, such as "probable cause," "preponderance of the evidence," and

6. Paul Ricoeur, "The Model of the Text: Meaningful Action Considered as a Text," *Social Research 38* (1971), no. 3, Fall, 529–62. Reprinted in Paul Ricoeur, *Hermeneutics and the Human Sciences*, ed. John B. Thompson (Cambridge: Cambridge University Press, 1981): 197–221.

7. Ibid., 215.

"beyond a reasonable doubt." For Ricoeur, the task of philosophy is to avoid the skepticism that doubts everything while at the same time abandoning the ideal of total certainty.

In a special section at the end of the preface, Ricoeur explains to his readers why he omitted from this book two chapters which were originally part of the Gifford Lectures. They were called "The Self in the Mirror of the Scriptures" and "The Mandated Self." The first of these dealt with the naming of God through the Old and New Testaments. In the symbolic network of the Scriptures, we find the kerygmatic dimension distinguished from the argumentative mode of philosophy. The second lecture dealt with the narratives of "vocation," of the calling of the prophets and disciples, and the understanding of the self contained in the response to the call. "The relation between call and response was therefore the strong connection between these two lectures"(23).

Ricoeur omitted the lectures from this work for two reasons: (1) He wanted this book to be an autonomous philosophical discourse by putting into parentheses the convictions which tied him to his biblical faith. This has been a guiding principle in all of his philosophical work. (2) If Ricoeur has defended his work from becoming a "crypto-theology," he also defends biblical faith from becomming a "crypto-philosophy." In particular, he does not want biblical faith to replace the *cogito* as a form of foundation against which his hermeneutics has fought continually.

Personal Identity

RICOEUR BEGINS his studies of the self by looking at the linguistic means at our disposal to identify anything, to refer to individual things and pick them out of a group of similar things. He claims that a person is, at the lowest level possible, "one of the things that we distinguish by means of identifying reference"(27). He will begin with a linguistic study of the operations of individualization found in natural languages. Definite descriptions create a class with a single member (e.g., the first man to walk on the moon), while proper names refer to a single individual without, however, giving any information about the individual (e.g., Socrates). The third category of individualizing operators is made up of pronouns (e.g., you, he) and deictics such as demonstratives (e.g. this one, that one), adverbs of time and place (e.g. now, then, here, there), and the tenses of verbs. These operators individualize with reference to the speaker. "Here" means in the proximity of the speaker, in relation to which "there" makes sense. "Now" refers to events contemporaneous with the speaking itself. At this point, none of these individualizing operations privileges the person.

In moving from the identification of any kind of particular to the identification of persons, Ricoeur follows P. F. Strawson, who in his book *Individuals*[8] claims that there are only two kinds of basic particulars, things (physical objects) and persons. Every identification refers ultimately to one of these two classes of individuals. At this point, what is important are the sets of predicates appropriate to each basic particular.

Strawson's second main thesis is that the first basic particular is the body, or physical object, because it satisfies the criterion of having a unique spatio-temporal location. Persons are also bodies, but they, unlike bodies, are a referent for two series of predicates, physical and psychological. The importance of this claim is that souls (à la Descartes), ideas, percepts, etc. are not fundamental or basic particulars. This cuts off any temptation to relapse into subjectivism or idealism. It also means that the person cannot be considered as a pure consciousness to which is added a body, as is the case in classical mind/body dualisms. The importance of this double attribution of predicates to *the same thing* is that we eliminate any double reference to body and soul by two series of predicates.

The first study follows one of the two linguistic approaches to the problem of the self, that of identifying reference. In the second chapter, Ricoeur takes up the other approach, enunciation, or speech-acts. Speech-acts immediately involve the "I" and the "you" of interlocution, whereas referential identification is centered on the "he." "The question will be finally to determine how the 'I you' of interlocution can be externalized in a 'him' or a 'her' without losing its capacity to designate itself, and how the 'he/she' of identifying reference can be internalized in a speaking subject who designates himself or herself as an I"(41).

The theory of speech-acts, begun by Austin and perfected by Searle, is well known. A fundamental element of the theory is the distinction between performatives and constatives. The latter describe a state of affairs; the former are speech-actions, where the saying is the doing itself. Their paradigm illustration is a promise, where saying "I promise you" is to make a promise and not to describe a promise. Other examples would be rendering a verdict, making a proclamation, naming a child, etc. The importance of this is that it is a principal intersection between the theory of language and the theory of action. Secondly, reflexive speech implies both an "I" who speaks and a "you" to whom the speech is addressed. "In short, utterance equals interlocution"(44).

Action and Agent

THE NEXT TWO chapters link up the linguistic analysis of identifying reference and speech-acts with the philosophy of action. In chapter 3, Ricoeur

8. P. F. Strawson, *Individuals* (London: Methuen, 1959).

deals with the concepts in the philosophy of action, devoid of reference to a particular agent. The following chapter introduces the imputation of agency. "What does action, we shall ask, teach about its agent? And to what extent can what is learned in this way contribute to clarifying the difference between *ipse* and *idem?*"(56).

At the level of identifying reference, the network of concepts with which we describe action refers to an agent as *being spoken about*. But this is far different from an explicit self-imputation of an action to an agent. Only at the end of Ricoeur's next chapter will we see the interrelationship between identifying reference and self-designation of an "acting subject."

For the purposes of this study, Ricoeur puts "in parentheses" the unifying principle of chains of actions, that is, the "practical unities of a higher order." These include techniques, skilled crafts, arts, games, all of which order chains of actions so that some actions are understood as parts of higher-order actions. This means that at this point he will set aside ethical predicates which evaluate actions, or chains of actions, as good, just, etc.

Action and agent belong to the same conceptual schema; this includes concepts such as motive, circumstance, intention, deliberation, voluntary, constraint, intended consequences, and so forth. The important thing is they they form a coherent network such that one must understand how all of them function and what they mean, in order to understand any one of them. The network as a whole determines what will "count as" an action. One way of seeing this network is that it constitutes the list of questions that can be asked of an agent about an action: when, under what circumstances, with what intention, why (what motive), what influences, and so forth.

Within the framework of identifying reference, the question "Who?" can be answered with a proper name, a demonstrative, or a definite description. Ricoeur believes that analytic philosophy of action has created problems for itself by focusing its discussion on the question of what will count as an action among the *events which happen in the world*. This has led it to couple the question "What?" with the question "Why?" such that distinguishing between an action and an event depends on the mode of explanation of the action (the "why?"). "The use of 'why?' in the explanation of action thus becomes the arbiter of the description of what counts as action"(61).[9]

Ricoeur now looks at the analytic philosophy of action as it interprets the meaning of "intention." The fundamental and guiding question in this view is "what distinguishes intentional actions from unintentional ones?" Anscombe's answer is that actions are intentional if a certain sense of "because" applies to

9. See R. S. Peters, *The Concept of Motivation* (London: Routledge and Kegan Paul, 1958).

them. This sense is that the *because* gives a "reason for acting"(69). This opens a whole range of answers to "why?" which are mixed or even counterexamples. Aristotle reminds us that in some cases the question "why?" doesn't have any sense: cases where the action was the result of ignorance or of constraint. Ricoeur claims that the main victim of this kind of analysis is the dichotomy between reason for acting and cause. He says that there is a whole spectrum of answers to "why?" and only at the far extremes of the spectrum do you find a pure opposition between reason and cause. In the case of "backward-looking" motives such as vengeance, the line between cause and reason is completely erased. He concludes, "But one can see how fluid the border is between reason-for-acting, forward-looking motive, mental cause, and cause as such (a grimacing face made me jump). The criterion of the question 'why?' is therefore firm; its application suprisingly flexible" (69).

According to Ricoeur, the analytic philosophy of action has been preoccupied with the question "What-why?" to the exclusion of the question "who?". He says, "In my opinion, it is the exclusive concern with the truth of the description that tends to overshadow any interest in assigning the action to its agent"(72). This is the same reason that analytic philosophy has neglected the sense of intention as "intending-to," the present intention to do something in the future. The dilemma is that the truth of such an intention claim rests on the nonverifiable declaration of the agent, or leads to a theory of internal mental events. For Ricoeur, only a phenomenology of attestation can account for "intending-to." The criterion of truth is not the verifiability of a description, but the confidence in a testimony. Even a declared intention belongs to the category of a shared confession and not to the category of a public description. In conclusion, the "intention-to," relegated to the third rank by conceptual analysis of the type done by Anscombe, finds itself in the first rank from the phenomenological perspective. This is because this sense of intention is very close to the act of promising.

In Ricoeur's first three chapters, the question *who?* was eclipsed by semantic considerations of the pair *what/why?*. In chapter 4, he returns to the central focus of *who?*, or the relation between the agent and the action. Earlier studies concentrated on distinguishing actions from events and on the relationship between intentional explanations and causal explanations. In returning to the role of the agent, Ricoeur recalls the theses of Strawson, discussed in his first chapter, and the linguistic act of *ascription*. Strawson's principal theses are that persons are "basic particulars" and all attribution of predicates is of persons or bodies; certain predicates are attributable only to persons and they are not reducible to any one or any set of predicates attributable to bodies. Secondly, we attribute both body predicates and person predicates to the *same* thing, i.e., persons. Finally, mental predicates are attributable to ourselves and others without having a different meaning.

Turning his attention to contemporary theory of action, Ricoeur wants to show that ascription has a different meaning than attribution. Each term in the network of action (*what? why?*), refers back to the *who?*. When we speak of the action, we ask who did it. When we ask for the motive, we refer directly to the agent. Ricoeur notes that these inquiries are not symmetrical: the question "who?" is answered when we name or otherwise indicate the agent; the search for motives is interminable.

Ricoeur asks why contemporary philosophy of action has resisted any kind of profound analysis of the relation between the action and the agent. He gives two reasons: Much of the discussion is dominated by an ontology of events (Davidson) and other analyses are dominated by an ontology of "things in general" (Strawson).

Ricoeur rejects, however, the claim that moral or judicial imputation of an action to an agent is merely a strong form of ascription. The first reason is that moral imputation makes no sense in cases of banal actions or simple acts disconnected from a practice or a complex human action. Secondly, imputation properly applies only in cases of actions which are praiseworthy or blamable. But to condemn an action is to submit it to an accusatory process of the "verdictive" type. The third reason is that imputation is on a different level from the self-designation of a speaker because it implies the *power to act*, including the causal efficacy—however explained—of this power.

But what does "power to act" mean? The *third problem* arises from the fact that "to say that an action depends on its agent is to say in an equivalent fashion that it is in the agent's power"(101). With an analysis of the "power to act," efficient causality, ejected from physics by Galileo, rediscovers its native land: the experience we all have of the power to act. Ricoeur claims that this experience is a "primitive fact." This does not mean it is a given or a starting point, but that it will be seen as such at the *end* of a dialectic. The dialectic will have a disjunctive phase, where efficient causality implied in the power to act is seen as different and disconnected from other forms of causality. It will have also a conjunctive phase where the primitive causality of the agent is shown to be connected with other forms of causality.

Ricoeur proposes an ontology of the *lived body* [*corps propre*], "that is, of *a* body which is also *my* body and which, by its double allegiance to the order of physical bodies and to that of persons, therefore lies at the point of articulation of the power to act which is ours and of the course of things which belongs to the world order"(111). So, the power of acting is rooted in a phenomenology of the "I can" and the ontology of the "lived body."

Narrative Identity

UP TO THIS POINT, Ricoeur limited his discussion to semantic and pragmatic considerations of the theory of language and theory of action with respect to the constitution of the self as self-designation and as agent of an action. At the end of his analyses, he reintroduced the phenomenological concept of a "lived body" as the intermediary between action and agent. All of this served as a "propaedeutic to the question of selfhood [*ipséité*]"(113). The most serious omission in all of the previous studies has been the dimension of temporality: "The person of whom we are speaking and the agent on whom the action depends have a history, are their own history"(113). In addition, the whole problematic of *personal identity* has been omitted. To tie these two themes together, considering the contemporary debates in Anglo-American philosophy about personal identity, Ricoeur will introduce the dialectic between *sameness (mêmeté)* and *selfhood (ipséité)* and the central idea of narrative identity. Once he has been able to show the advantages of this narrative identity in resolving the paradoxes of the problem of personal identity, he can finally turn to the thesis stated in his introduction, "namely that narrative theory finds one of its major justifications in the role it plays as a middle ground between the descriptive viewpoint on action, to which we have confined ourselves until now, and the prescriptive viewpoint which will prevail in the studies that follow. A triad has thus imposed itself on my analysis: describe, narrate, prescribe—each moment of the triad implying a specific relation between the constitution of action and the constitution of the self"(114–15). Narrative already contains, even in its most descriptive mode, evaluations, estimations, and value judgments. In this sense, it serves as a preparation for ethics proper.

It is here that Ricoeur clearly lays out the two meanings of identity and begins to show their dialectical relationship. In one sense, identity means *sameness;* its other sense is *selfhood.* The context for this discussion of identity is permanence through time. What does it mean to say that someone or something is identical at two different times? On the most basic level, identity means numerical identity—there is one and the same thing, rather than two or more different things. Another sense of identity is qualitative, or the substitutablity of one thing for another. Determining identity in cases separated by time, as in cases of law where we claim that the defendant is *the same person* as the person who committed the crime, can be very difficult. This leads to a third sense of identity, that of uninterrupted continuity between two stages of development of what we take to be the same individual. This kind of identity overcomes the problem of a lack of sameness or similarity required in the qualitative sense of identity. Another sense is permanence in time represented by, say, a genetic code, or a structure, or the organization of a combinatory system. All of these meanings of identity are tied in some way to the idea of *sameness.*

The question now is whether selfhood implies a form of permanence in time which does not depend on a substratum of sameness. What we are looking for, says Ricoeur, is "a form of permanence in time that is a reply to the question 'Who am I?'"(118). His proposal is that there are two models for this kind of identity, *character* and *keeping a promise*. In the first case, identity in the sense of one's character is very close to identity in the sense of sameness, an enduring and reidentifiable substratum. In the second case, the selfhood implied in keeping promises is antithetical to sameness. For example, I say that even though I have different opinions, values, desires, inclinations, I will keep my word.

But what does "character" mean? "By 'character' I understand the set of distinctive marks which permit the reidentification of a human individual as being the same"(119). This will include all of the descriptive traits of "sameness" such as "qualitative identity, uninterrupted continuity and permanence in time."(119) Ricoeur reminds us that he has dealt at length with the concept of character in two of his previous works. In *Freedom and Nature*, character was seen as an absolutely permanent and involuntary aspect of our experience (along with our birth and our unconscious) to which we could, at most, consent.[10] It was the non-chosen perspective on our values and our capabilities. In *Fallible Man*, character represented a finite restriction on my openness to the world of things, ideas, values, and persons.[11] In the present work, Ricoeur wants to modify his view of character by situating it within the dialectic of identity. What is at issue is the immutability of character which he took as a given in his previous works. "Character, I would say today, designates the set of lasting dispositions by which a person is recognized"(121). Here, sameness is constitutive of selfhood.

But if identity in terms of sameness and identity in terms of selfhood find convergence in the idea of character, they are seen as divergent in the analysis of a promise kept. To keep a promise is not to remain the same through time but to defy the changes wrought by time. "Even if my desire were to change, even if I were to change my opinion or my inclination, 'I will hold firm'"(124). So the dialectic of sameness and selfhood has two poles: character, where sameness and permanence of dispositions constitute selfhood; and promising, where selfhood is maintained in spite of change, or in the absence of sameness. Ricoeur thinks that narrative identity is the mediating concept.

His thesis is that the true nature of narrative identity is found only in the dialectic of sameness and selfhood, and the dialectic itself is the main contribution

10. Paul Ricoeur, *Freedom and Nature: The Voluntary and the Involuntary*, trans. E. Kohak (Evanston: Northwestern University Press, 1966): 355–73. Translation of *Le Volontaire et l'involontaire* (Paris: Aubier, 1950).

11. Paul Ricoeur, *Fallible Man*, trans. C. Kelbey (Chicago: Henry Regnery, 1965): 77–98. Translation of *L'Homme faillible* (Paris: Aubier, 1960).

of the narrative theory to the constitution of the self. His arguments are in two steps: First, in an analysis of emplotment (*mise en intrigue*) along the same lines as we found in *Time and Narrative*, the construction of a narrative plot integrates diversity, variability, and discontinuity into the permanence in time. In short, it unifies elements that appear to be totally disparate. Secondly, this same emplotment, transferred from action to characters—characters in a narrative as distinct from "character" as a fundamental element of the existing individual—creates a dialectic of sameness and selfhood.

After giving a brief description of *configuration*, one of the principal concepts in *Time and Narrative*, Ricoeur undertakes to compare narrative configuration with impersonal description. He claims that narration occupies a middle place between description and prescription. He must now show its relation to both end-terms.

One touchstone of the difference between narrative and description is the role of *event*. On the one hand, an event appears to be totally contingent, and thus from the narrative point of view, a discordance. On the other hand, it advances the narrative and is seen as necessary to it. Thus, it is a concordance. The paradox of narration is that it transforms contingent events into necessary episodes by providing a context or link with other events.

Narrative identity has as its challenge to create a dynamic identity out of Locke's incompatible categories of identity and diversity. Ricoeur's thesis here is, "that the identity of the character is comprehensible through the transfer to the character of the operation of emplotment, first applied to the action recounted; characters, we will say, are themselves plots"(143). But what is the relation between character and narrated action? The personage has a unity and an identity correlative to those of the narrative itself. This is captured in the concept of a *role*. Our understanding of a narrative is that it is about agents and victims (*patients*). Ricoeur says, "For my part, I never forget to speak of humans as acting and suffering"(144–45). This shows, I think, the close relation between narration and ethics.

What is the relation between narrative identity and ethics, between narrating and prescribing? In the first case, narration always deals with actions that are "subject to approval or disapproval and agents that are subject to praise or blame"(164). Ricoeur also says that literature is a grand laboratory of the imagination where experiments are conducted in the realm of good and evil.

In the narrative dialectic of the character, one pole is the character, a constant set of dispositions which remains the same across time. The other pole is the self-constancy represented by commitment made and kept. In the ethical version of the dialectic of identity, character is in the role of sameness: this is what is identifiable and reidentifiable in me, through time and across all of my experiences and actions. The pole of selfhood, or identity in spite of diversity, is responsibility, or acting in such a manner that others can *count* on me and thus make me *accountable* for my actions. Narrative identity is between the poles of sameness as character and selfhood as responsibility.

Ethics and Morals

AT THIS POINT, Ricoeur begins his extensive discussion of the moral and ethical dimension of selfhood which is added to the linguistic, practical, and narrative aspects discussed previously. The guiding questions for these four groups of inquiries are: "Who is speaking? Who is acting? Who is telling his or her story? Who is the moral subject of imputation?"(169). The key predicates here will be "good" and "obligatory." Ricoeur says, "The ethical and moral determinations of action will be treated here as predicates of a new kind, and their relation to the subject of action as a new mediation along the return path to the self"(169).

But what is the difference between the terms "ethical" and "moral" for Ricoeur? He wants to distinguish between what is "considered to be good" and what "imposes itself as obligatory." "It is, therefore, by convention that I reserve the term 'ethics' for the *aim* of an accomplished life and the term 'morality' for the articulation of this aim in *norms* characterized at once by the claim to universality and an effect of constraint (later I shall say what links these two features together)"(170). From a historical point of view, we see the ethical concern of Aristotle in the *teleological* interest in the "good life." The moral point of view is found in Kant's *deontology*. In this chapter, Ricoeur seeks to establish the primacy of ethics over morals, the necessity for the goal of ethics to pass through the screen of norms (moral rules), and the recourse of such norms to the ethical goal. "In other words, according to the working hypothesis I am proposing, morality is held to constitute only a limited, although legitimate and even indispensable, actualization of the ethical aim, and ethics in this sense would then encompass morality"(170). But what is the relation between these terms and selfhood? Ricoeur answers, "To the ethical aim will correspond what we shall henceforth call self-esteem, and to the deontological moment, self-respect"(171).

Ricoeur argues at length for the primacy of ethics over morals. But what is the goal of ethics (*visée éthique*)? "Let us define 'ethical intention' as *aiming at the 'good life' with and for others, in just institutions*"(172). The "good life" is the aim of ethics. If we distinguish between practices and a "life-plan," the former are lower on the scale than the latter and their integration is found in the narrative unity of a life. In this discussion, which is well-centered on Aristotle's *Nicomachean Ethics*, there is a hierarchy in which practices, including professions, games, and art, are subordinate to the idea of "the good life." The linkage with self-esteem is the following: Our practices are defined by constitutive rules and standards of excellence. In appreciating the excellence or success in our actions, we begin to appreciate ourselves as the author of those actions. Ricoeur points out that "life" in the expression "good life" does not have a biological meaning as much as a social meaning that was familiar to the Greeks. They spoke of a "life of pleasure," a "political life," a "contemplative life," etc. For Ricoeur, "life" has this sense as well as the notion of the rootedness of our lives in the biological sense of "to live." Finally, it is in the narrative unity of a life that the estimations applied to particular actions and the evaluation of persons themselves are joined together. In fact, Ricoeur claims that there is a sort of "hermeneutical circle" between our lives as a whole under the idea of the "good life," and our most important particular choices, such as career, spouse, leisure pursuits, etc. But this is not the only hermeneutical connection. "For the agent, interpreting the text of an action is interpreting himself or herself"(179). A bit further, Ricoeur says, "On the ethical plane, self-interpretation becomes self-esteem. In return, self-esteem follows the fate of interpretation"(179).

If the "good life" is the goal of ethics, it is lived with and for others. This becomes the basis for the second part of Ricoeur's reflection on ethics. He designates this concern for the other as *solicitude*. It is not something added to self-esteem from the outside but is an internal, dialogical dimension "such that self-esteem and solicitude cannot be experienced or reflected upon one without the other"(180). Self-esteem is not founded on accomplishment but on capacity; the ability to judge (to esteem) is based on the ability to act (*le pouvoir-faire*). "The question is then whether the mediation of the other is not required along the route from capacity to realization"(181). The importance of this question is found in certain political theories in which individuals have rights independently of any social connections and the role of the state is relegated to protecting antecedently existing rights. According to Ricoeur, this view rests on a misunderstanding of the role of the other as a mediator between capacity and effectuation. For Aristotle, friendship (*amitié*) plays a mediating role between the goal of the good life found in self-esteem, a solitary virtue, and justice, a political virtue. Friendship introduces the notion of "mutuality." "Friendship, however, is not justice, to the extent that the latter governs institutions and the former interpersonal relations"(184). Equality is presupposed in our relations of friendship, while it is a goal to be achieved in our political institutions. Ricoeur thus takes from Aristotle "the ethics of reciprocity, of sharing, of living together"(187). Self-esteem is the reflexive moment of the goal of the good life, while the relation between the self and the other is characterized by solicitude, which is based on the exchange of giving and receiving. For Ricoeur, this shows the primacy of the ethical goal of the good life, including solicitude for the other, over the moral claims of obligation. As he says, friendship involves reciprocity, while the moral injunction is asymmetrical.

The inverse of the moral injunction is *suffering*. "Suffering is not defined solely by physical pain, nor even by mental pain, but by the reduction, even the destruction, of the capacity for acting, of being-able-to-act, experienced as a violation of self-integrity"(190). Ricoeur sees this as laid out on a spectrum ranging from the injunction coming from the other ("Thou shalt not . . . ") to the opposite end, where sympathy for the suffering other comes from the self. Friendship lies in the middle of this spectrum where the self and the other share an equality and a common wish to live together. The mutuality of friendship means that the roles are reversible, while the persons who play these roles are not substitutable. Ricoeur puts it this way: "The agents and patients of an action are caught up in relationships of exchange which, like language, join together the reversibility of roles and nonsubstitutability of persons. Solicitude adds the dimension of value, whereby each person is *irreplaceable* in our affection and our esteem"(193).

The ideas of irreplaceability and nonsubstitutability lead to the notion of *similitude*, as the result of the exchange between self-esteem and solicitude for the other. This means that, finally, I understand the other as a self, an agent and author of his actions, who has reasons for his actions, who can rank his preferences, etc. All of our ethical feelings, says Ricoeur, refer back to this phenomenology of the "you, too" and "like me." "Fundamentally equivalent are the esteem of the *other as oneself* and the esteem of *oneself as an other*"(194).

But Ricoeur wants to extend his analysis of the ethical goal of the good life from interpersonal relations to institutions, and he extends the virtue of solicitude for the other to the virtue of justice. By "institution," Ricoeur means those structures of *living together* found in historical communities, structures that extend beyond simple interpersonal relations but are bound up with the latter through their function of the distribution of roles, responsibilities, privileges, goods, and rewards. Ricoeur asks if justice is found on the level of ethics and teleology or, as Rawls and Kant would have it, only on the deontological level of morals. Ricoeur's own answer is that justice has two sides: the side of the *good* which is an extension of interpersonal relations, and the *legal* side where it implies a judicial system of coherent laws. He is concerned in this chapter with the first sense or aspect of justice.

But what is the relation between the institution, as an abstract organization of distribution of goods and burdens, and the individuals who make up social institutions? Ricoeur says, "The conception of society as a system of distribution transcends the terms of the opposition. The institution as regulation of the distribution of roles, hence as a system, is indeed something more and something other than the individuals who play those roles. . . . An institution considered as a rule of distribution exists only to the extent that individuals take part in it"(200). Distributive justice is not a matter of mere arithmetical equality among individuals but a *proportional* equality which relates merit to each individual. In conclusion, Ricoeur says that justice adds equality to solicitude and its range is all humanity rather than interpersonal relations. This is why he adds "in just institutions" to our ethical pursuit of the "good life" lived "with and for others."

Let us sum up the argument so far. At the beginning, Ricoeur announced three theses that he would treat in successive studies: "(1) the primacy of ethics over morality, (2) the necessity for the ethical aim to pass through the sieve of the norm, and (3) the legitimacy of recourse by the norm to the aim whenever the norm leads to impasses in practice"(170). We have just dealt with the primacy of ethics over morality. Let us now consider how Ricoeur deals with the question of the relation between the goal of ethics (teleology) and moral norms (deontology).

The criterion of universality is the hallmark of Kant's formalism. It is anticipated in Aristotle by the "golden mean" which characterizes all virtues. Aristotle's "good life" is approached by Kant's "good will, good without reservation." But the teleological character of "good" is lost when Kant adds "without reservation." What is more, for Kant it is the *will* which receives the predicate "good." As Ricoeur says, "the will, however, takes the place in Kantian morality that rational desire occupied in Aristotelian ethics; desire is recognized through its aim, will through its relation to law"(206).

Universality is the "royal road" to Kant's view of moral obligation. It is closely linked with "restraint" and through the latter with the idea of *duty*. Kant's genius was to place in the same person the power to command and the power to obey or disobey the command. The moral law is an "autonomous," a universal law of reason that the autonomous subject gives himself. At the same time, his autonomy means that he can choose to obey or disobey this law. But this freedom, this autonomy, is affected by the propensity to evil. What effect does this propensity have on the status of the autonomy of the will? Ricoeur says that there are two important ideas here: (1) that evil, taken back to the origin of the maxims, should be thought of in terms of a real opposition; (2) that in radicalizing evil, Kant radicalized the idea of free will. Ricoeur concludes, "Because there is evil, the aim of the 'good life' has to be submitted to the test of moral obligation"(218).

Ricoeur has already shown how solicitude for the other was implicitly contained in the idea of self-esteem; he wants to show now that respect for others is implicit in the idea of obligation, rule, or law. His argument is that respect owed to others is tied to solicitude on the level of ethics; and, that on the level of morality, it is in the same relation to autonomy that solicitude is to the goal of the good life on the ethical level. In fact, Ricoeur claims that this relation will help us see the relation between the first formulation of the categorical imperative, in terms of obligation, and the second formulation, which tells us to respect others as ends-in-themselves. He has previously distinguished between the *power to act* which is the capacity for an agent to be the author of his actions, and *power-in-common* which is the capacity of the members of a community to will to live together. This latter capacity is to be distinguished from the relation of domination, which is the source of political violence. Political violence can take many forms, from constraint to torture and even to murder. In torture, it is the self-respect of the victim which is broken. Ricoeur says that all of these figures of evil are answered by the "no" of morality. This is why so many moral norms are expressed in the negative, "Thou shalt not. . . ."

The second part of his argument concerning respect for others is to show its relation to solicitude. The Golden Rule, he says, is in an intermediary role between solicitude and Kant's second formulation of the categorical imperative in terms of respect for persons. He asks, "What, indeed, is it to treat humanity in my person and in the person of others as a *means,* if not to exert *upon* the will of others that power which, full of restraint in the case of influence, is unleashed in all forms that violence takes, culminating in torture?"(225).

Ricoeur has claimed that justice is a virtue principally of institutions. He now takes justice, in the sense of distributive justice, as the key intersection between the goal of ethics and the deontological point of view. But the very term "justice" is ambiguous. One sense emphasizes separation, in the sense of what belongs to me does not belong to you. Justice is to determine what should belong to whom. Another sense, however, puts the emphasis on cooperation and the community of interests. Related to these two senses of justice is the ambiguity between two senses of "equal": as in arithmetic, where all parts are exactly the same, and as proportional, where the parts to be distributed are proportional to some other measure such as merit, social standing, or power.

There have been many attempts to establish the principles of justice, especially on the social level. One of the most enduring is the "social contract," where justice is founded on a contract between individuals who, by this contract, create a community and establish the rules for the distribution of goods and obligations, rights and privileges, duties and burdens. Ricoeur sees an analogy between the role of this contract on the level of institutions and the place of autonomy on the level of morality: "a freedom sufficiently disengaged from the gangue of inclinations provides a law for itself which is the very law of freedom"(229). At this point, Ricoeur turns to a long analysis of Rawls' attempt to establish the principles of justice through a theoretical and hypothetical gambit known as the "veil of ignorance." Rawls asks, what would be the principles of justice in a community if the members of the community could write those rules *not knowing what their actual lot would be?* His idea of justice as "fairness" leads, through this thought-experiment, to two general principles of justice: First, equal freedoms of citizenship, such as freedom of expression, etc.; second, a principle of difference which tells us under which circumstances inequalities are acceptable.

Ricoeur claims that what Rawls has done is to formalize a sense of justice which is already presupposed. Rawls himself agrees that he is not establishing a completely independent meaning of justice, that he relies on our precomprehension of what is just and unjust. What he does claim is that there is a "reflected equilibrium" between his theory and our "considered convictions." We do indeed have certain convictions about justice and injustice (e.g., religious intolerance, torture) which seem certain, while others such as the distribution of wealth or power seem less sure. Rawls' arguments are of the same type as those of Kant when he tries to prove the necessity for universalization of maxims. "The whole system of argumentation can therefore be seen as a progressive rationalization of these convictions, when they are affected by prejudices or weakened by doubts. This rationalization consists in a complex process of mutual adjustment between conviction and theory"(237).

At the end of his analysis of Rawls' attempt to establish a contractual basis for institutional justice, Ricoeur says that we can draw two conclusions: (1) We can see how the attempt to give a purely procedural foundation for institutional justice takes to the maximum the ambition to free the deontological point of view of morality from the teleological perspective of ethics. (2) Yet we also see that this attempt clearly shows the limits of this ambition. In short, formalism has tried to banish inclinations from the sphere of rational will, the treatment of others as means in the interpersonal realm, and utilitarianism in the sphere of institutions. Instead, the deontological point of view insists on "autonomy in the first sphere, the person as end in himself in the second, and the social contract in the third"(238). The social contract plays the same role on the level of institutions as autonomy on the level of morality. But the social contract is a *fiction,* a "founding fiction, to be sure, but a fiction nonetheless"(239). Ricoeur criticizes social contract theories on the grounds that they are plausible only because we have forgotten our fundamental desire to live together. The foundation of deontology, in other words is, Ricoeur claims, found in *"the desire to live well with and for others in just institutions"*(239).

The third part of Ricoeur's reflections on ethics is to show how a morality of deontological norms must return to the fundamental insight of a teleological ethics in order to resolve the aporias arising in the application of the universal norms to difficult practical cases. His guiding thesis is that an ethics of obligation "produces conflictual situations where practical wisdom has no recourse, in our opinion, other than to return to the initial intuition of ethics, in the framework of moral judgment in situation; that is, to the vision or aim of the 'good life' with and for others in just institutions"(240). There are two possible misinterpretations to avoid here: First, we do not need to resort to any kind of Hegelian *Sittlichkeit*, or superior moment, which surpasses both the morality of obligation and the ethical goal of the good life. Second, the return from a morality of obligation to ethics should not be taken as a rejection of the morality of obligation. What Ricoeur is looking for, in other words, is a "practical wisdom" which allows us to decide in difficult particular cases without falling into a kind of arbitrary situationism.

At this point, Ricoeur resorts to a very unusual variation of style, reminiscent of Nietzsche, by inserting a nine-page *Interlude* called "Tragic Action." It is dedicated to his late son, Olivier, who died at the age of thirty-nine, only days after Ricoeur finished the Gifford Lectures in Edinburgh. Ricoeur takes as a case of "the tragedy of action," the moral conflict at the heart of Sophocles' *Antigone*. Antigone follows the "unwritten law" to bury her brother, Polynices, who was killed in an uprising against Thebes. She disobeys the direct order of the king, Creon, who has commanded that Polynices not be buried because he was a traitor to the city. For Creon, the moral rules are strict and easy: Only that which serves the city is good, that which harms it is evil. But Antigone is driven by the conviction that she is obliged, by unwritten laws, to provide a decent burial for her brother. Ricoeur says, "But in invoking them [the unwritten laws] to found her intimate conviction, she posited the limit that points up the human, all too human, character of every institution"(245). It is just such a limit which leads to ethics being instructed by tragedy. Once again, Ricoeur's thesis is that the dialectic of ethics and morality is played out in the moral judgment in particular situations.

Moral formalism, in Kant's sense, is forced to rely on the intuition of ethics in three areas already discussed: the universal self, the plurality of persons, and the institutional environment. Ricoeur now takes these three areas up again in reverse order, beginning with institutions. In the preceding chapter, he had already shown the possibility of conflict inherent in the idea of justice as a "just distribution." In short, it is the diversity of *contributions*, whether individual or collective, that raises the problem of a just distribution of rights, roles, responsibilities, and goods. This problem had led Aristotle to his idea of "proportional justice." The importance of institutions for this solution is clear: Referring to his seventh study, Ricoeur says, "We then admitted that it was only in a specific institutional milieu that the capacities and predispositions that distinguish human action can blossom; the individual, we said then, becomes human only under the condition of certain institutions; and we added: if this is so, the obligation to serve these institutions is itself a condition for the human agent to continue to develop" (254–55). Now the political state is the set of practices organized around the distribution of power and domination. "Democracy," says Ricoeur, "is not a political system without conflicts but a system in which conflicts are open and negotiable in accordance with recognized rules of arbitration"(258). In response to the "crisis of legitimacy" of certain political institutions, he calls for the public recognition of traditions which make a place for tolerance and pluralism, "not out of concessions to external pressures, but out of inner conviction, even if this is late in coming"(261).

Ricoeur next considers the possibility of conflicts imbedded in the very nature of the second version of Kant's categorical imperative: the universality of humanity and the individuality of each person as an "end-in-himself." The conflict can arise between "respect for the law," which reflects universality, and "respect for persons," which reflects "the solicitude that is addressed to persons in their irreplaceable singularity"(262). Ricoeur holds that Kant does not see this possibility of conflict because he sees only the subsumption of the maxim under a rule. But it is when we consider the opposite direction, the application of the rule in concrete situations, where individuals demand to be recognized as ends-in-themselves, that we recognize the place of conflict. In the application of rules to particular situations, the rule is subject to the test of circumstances and consequences.

At this point, Ricoeur gives a summary analysis of promise-making and the obligation to keep promises. He says that it is the "you can count on me" of the promise which ties selfhood with the reciprocity for the other founded in solicitude. "Not keeping one's promise is betraying both the other's expectation and the institution that mediates the mutual trust of speaking subjects"(268). What Kant failed to see is the possibility of conflict between respect for the law and respect for persons. To illustrate the kind of conflict that is possible, Ricoeur takes cases from the "end of life" and the "beginning of life." For the first, he takes the case of the obligation to tell the truth to dying persons. This obligation is tempered by compassion for certain patients who are too weak to stand the truth or those for whom the clinical truth would become simply a death sentence.

For the second kind of case, Ricoeur takes the question of abortion. While admitting that on the basis of biological criteria, the embryo is a biological individual from the moment of conception, Ricoeur asks "whether practical wisdom, without entirely losing this biologic criterion from sight, must not take into account the phenomena of thresholds and stages that put into question the simple alternative between 'person' and 'thing'"(271). Ricoeur thinks that the dialectic between sameness and selfhood leads us away from any simplistic substantialist ontology operative here. An opposite kind of thesis is that personhood is established only by well-developed capacities, such that only well-educated and autonomous adults would qualify for the status of personhood. We could decide to protect lesser beings, like we protect animals or nature, but they would have no right to be respected. Ricoeur rejects this view as well because it is an "all-or-nothing" position which does not admit degrees or stages of development. He argues for a progression of qualitatively different rights tied to a progression of biological thresholds. What is called for in these kinds of cases is "critical solicitude," where our moral judgments are the result of the good counsel of wise and competent men and women.

Ricoeur continues his argument that there are conflicts in the very heart of the claims of morality which call for a return to the most basic insight of ethics. In particular, there is the continual possibility—and reality—of conflict between the universalist claims of the rules derived from moral principles and the "recognition of positive values belonging to the *historical and communitarian contexts* of the realization of these same rules"(274). Ricoeur's claim is that there would not be a place for the tragedy of action unless there were a place for both the universalist thesis and the contextualist thesis mediated by "the practical wisdom of moral judgment in situation"(274).

In order to argue for this thesis, Ricoeur says that we must first make an extended revision to Kantian formalism which will clearly show the universalist claim and will sharpen as much as possible its conflict with contextualism. He will make this revision in three steps: (1) Question the priority Kant gives to the principle of autonomy with respect to the plurality of individuals and the principle of justice as applied to institutions. Ricoeur thinks that the principle of autonomy should be at the end of the series, not at the beginning. (2) Question the restrictive use Kant makes of the criterion of universalization. According to Ricoeur, this criterion is very impoverished since it is limited to noncontradiction and ignores the idea of the coherence of a moral system. Such a coherence shows that such a formalism is not vacuous, in the sense that a whole series of moral obligations or rules can be derived from the single principle requiring respect for others; furthermore, these moral obligations are mutually coherent and not conflictual among themselves. Finally, these rules are such that inferior rules are coherent with superior rules. (3) Finally, Kant's formalism lies on the retrospective path of *justification,* while the real conflicts arise in the prospective direction of deriving judgments from rules and rules from principles, that is, in the application of universal principles to concrete cases. In sum, Ricoeur's goal is to show both the credibility of the demand for universalization *and* the contextual character of the application of moral rules.

It is, he says, the job of political practice to deal with this conflict and these perplexities. He seeks moreover to underline the importance of the *historicity* of these political choices.

Next, if we move from the political level to the level of interpersonal relations, a new dichotomy or conflict arises: the otherness (*altérité*) of individuals is opposed to the unitary aspect of the concept of humanity. There is a *schism*, between respect for the law and respect for persons. In short, there is again a conflict between universalism and contextualism. If we have a concept of justice which is purely procedural, an ethics of argumentation can resolve the conflicts. But is the situation the same with the principle of respect for persons? Is resorting to developmental biology to decide whether the fetus is a person, a thing, or something intermediary not similar to looking for the best arguments in a debate over the *rights* of the fetus? Ricoeur accepts this thesis, but only to a certain point. He is in favor of contextualist explanations but objects strenuously to "an apology of difference for the sake of difference which, finally, makes all differences indifferent, to the extent that it makes all discussion useless"(286). In other words, what Ricoeur rejects in an ethics of argumentation (representing the demand for universalization) is not the taking into account of circumstances in constructing the best argument, but its attempt at *purification.* Kant wanted to purify all moral arguments from any kind of inclination, desire, pleasure, happiness, etc., and today Habermas directs his purification to anything *conventional,* in order to free moral arguments from anything having to do with tradition and authority.

Ricoeur, on the contrary, suggests a reformulation of the ethics of argumentation that integrates the objections of contextualism with the demands of universalization. He wants to call into question the conflict between argumentation and convention and substitute a dialectic between *argumentation* and *conviction.* He says, "what do we discuss, if not the best way for each party in the great debate to aim, beyond institutional mediations, at a complete life lived with and for others in just institutions? The articulations that we never cease to reinforce between deontology and teleology finds its "highest—and most fragile—expression in *the reflective equilibrium between the ethics of argumentation and considered convictions*" (288–89). One aspect of practical wisdom is the "art of conversation, in which the ethics of argumentation is put to the test in the conflict of convictions"(290).

What is most important about Ricoeur's moral theory is that he does not accept the classical conflict between a teleological ethics and a nomological morality—to use his conventions—as an antinomy. He argues that they are poles in a dialectical relationship, each calling on the other to complete its vision of a moral universe. A teleological view of the goal of ethics needs universal moral rules as a necessary means; on the other hand, the application of these rules to dificult particular cases calls for an appeal to the ultimate *telos* of morality.

The dialectic between ethics as the teleological goal of "a good life lived with others in just institutions" and a morality of universal rules finds its mediation in "practical wisdom." This wisdom is precisely the application of moral rules to particular cases where a "conflict of convictions" is tempered by an ethics of argumentation. In his moral theory, Ricoeur replaces the "conflict of interpretations" of his hermeneutics with a conflict of convictions. In both cases, it is the task of reflective philosophy to adjudicate among the conflicting claims—each of which asserts that it is absolute.

Ontology of the Self

RICOEUR'S HERMENEUTICS of the self and its relation to the other actually ends with the ninth study. Ricoeur asks, however, "What kind of being is the self?" He says that his ontology of the self will be tentative and exploratory. He reminds us that the hermeneutics of the self was based on three successive problematics: reflection by the indirect route of analysis; the determination of selfhood by its contrast with sameness; and a second determination of selfhood through its dialectic with otherness. He calls the result of this progressive study a hermeneutics of the self through a triple mediation. In the previous studies the guiding principle has been the *polysemy* of the question "Who?": who speaks, who acts, who tells a story, who is responsible? But, beneath the structure organized around the question "Who?" is the substructure organized around the three problematics described above. The first four studies responded to reflection through analysis; the fifth and sixth dealt with the contrast between selfhood and sameness; and, the seventh, eighth, and ninth chapters focused on the dialectic between selfhood and the other.

Above all, Ricoeur wants to warn us again against any attempt to establish an epistemological—or ontological—foundation in the manner of Descartes or Husserl. Instead of any claim to absolute truth, he reminds us that attestation is a level of belief and confidence based on "testimony." It is not an attempt to create an auto-foundational certitude of a Cartesian *cogito,* and so it escapes the "humiliation of the cogito reduced to sheer illusion following the Nietzschean critique"(299). Analysis, in the sense used by analytic philosophy, *attests,* in Ricoeur's sense, to the ontological import of the self when, with Strawson, the basic individuals are bodies and persons, and, with Davidson, acts are construed as kinds of events. In these analyses, the self is that which is talked about. But hermeneutics renders a reciprocal service to analytical philosophy by showing that the self is not the result of some "linguistic mistake" or even more importantly, insisting on a referential aspect of language as a corrective for those philosophies such as French structuralism which refuse to "go outside" of language and mistrust any extralinguistic reality. Ricoeur says, "I find here again the sort of *ontological vehemence* whose advocate I have been elsewhere in the name of the conviction that—even in the uses of language that appear to be the least referential, as is the case with metaphor and narrative fiction—language expresses being, even if this ontological aim is as though postponed, deferred by the prior denial of the literal referentiality of ordinary language"(301).

An important difference between the being-true of attestation of Ricoeur and that of Aristotle is that the contrary of attestation is suspicion, while the contrary of being-true for Aristotle is being false. "Suspicion is also the path *toward* and crossing *within* attestation. It haunts attestation, as false testimony haunts true testimony. This adherence, this inherence of suspicion with respect to attestation, has marked the entire course of these studies"(302). To press on farther into the ontology of the self, Ricoeur says he must be more precise about selfhood, both in its difference from sameness and its relation to otherness.

The dialectic between selfhood and otherness is more fundamental than the relation between reflection and analysis and even the contrast betweeen selfhood and sameness. Otherness does not come from outside selfhood, but is part of the meaning and the ontological constitution of selfhood. He says that the phenomenological response to the meta-category of otherness is "the variety of experiences of passivity, intertwined in multiple ways in human action"(318). The main point of this dialectic is to prevent the self from pretending to occupy the place of a foundation. Otherness is joined to selfhood. The passivity at the core of otherness is manifested in three ways: "First, there is the passivity represented by the experience of one's own body—or better, as we shall say later, of the *flesh*—as mediator between the self and a world. . . . Next, we find the passivity implied by the relation of the self to the *foreign*, in the precise sense of the other (than) self. . . . Finally, we have the most deeply hidden passivity, that of the relation of the self to itself, which is *conscience*"(318). All three of these manifestations exhibit the complexity and density of the concept of otherness.

If, to use Strawson's terms, persons are also bodies, it is to the extent that each person is for himself his own body. The double belonging of the lived body to the order of things as well as to the self is echoed in Davidson's account of action as also an event. Ricoeur certainly includes suffering in the passivity of the body. He says, "With the variety of these degrees of passivity, one's own body is revealed to be the mediator between the intimacy of the self and the externality of the world"(322). The "flesh" is the place of the experience of passivity. Selfhood implies a "lived" otherness, of which the flesh is the foundation. In a powerful analogy, Ricoeur says,

The problem we called the reinscription of phenomenological time in cosmological time in *Time and Narrative* finds a series of equivalences here: just as it was necessary to invent the calendar to correlate the lived now with the anonymous instant and to draw up the geographic map to correlate the charnel here with an indifferent place, and thereby to inscribe the proper name—my name—in the civil register, it is necessary, as Husserl himself states, to *make* the flesh part of the world (*mondaneiser*) if it is to appear as a body among bodies (326).

97

Ricoeur goes on to speak of an otherness constitutive of the self and says that it gives full force to the paradoxical expression "oneself as another"(327).

The second category of the experience of the passivity of the self is in the "otherness" of other people. Ricoeur introduces the idea of a dialectic between self-esteem and friendship. He says that justice is generally considered in the sense of distributive justice in exchanges, but it could be rewritten in terms of a dialectic of action and affection. In the dialectic between the self and the other, it is the face of the other that appears to me and says, "Thou shalt not kill." It is the other who constitutes me as responsible, that is, capable of answering. "In this way, the word of the other comes to be placed at the origin of my acts"(336). So, self-designation which imputes moral responsiblity for my acts to me has its origin outside of the self.

The next pages are a debate between Kant and Levinas. Kant puts respect for the law above respect for other persons; Levinas says that the face of the other singularizes the commandment. To be effective, however, the voice of the other must become my voice; his command must become my conviction. This dialectic between the self and the other was already anticipated in Ricoeur's discussion of promising: "If another were not counting on me, would I be capable of keeping my word, of maintaining myself?"(341).

Ricoeur says that among the most *suspect* ideas are those of the "bad" or "good" conscience. A discussion of conscience will give him, he says, a perfect opportunity to put to the test his thesis that "attestation of selfhood is inseparable from an exercise of *suspicion*"(341). Even if we overcome the distinction between "good" and "bad" conscience, we must still deal with phenomena of *injunction* and *debt* which are ingrained in the idea of conscience. There are three challenges to overcome in order to rescue the concept of conscience from Nietzsche's attack.

First challenge. The conscience is the place where illusions about oneself are mixed with the truth of attestation. After an extended discussion of Nietzsche's analyses of the concept of conscience, Ricoeur says that the force of Nietzsche's method of suspicion is that all conscience is "bad conscience." The trap, says Ricoeur, is the danger of a new dogmatism. In order to return to the idea of conscience, we must abandon the ideas of "good" and "bad" conscience and go back to a kind of nonmoral suspicion which is the other face of attestation.

Second challenge. What happens when we "de-moralize" the conscience? How do we keep from falling back into the trap of "good" and "bad" conscience? Ricoeur says, "A remark made earlier with respect to the metaphor of the *court* puts us on the right path. Is it not because the stage of morality has been dissociated from the triad ethics-morality-conviction, then hypostasized because of this dissociation, that the phenomenon of conscience has been correlatively impoverished and the revealing metaphor of the voice has been eclipsed by the stifling metaphor of the court?"(351). Ricoeur says that the first injunction is a call to live well with and for others in just institutions. It is because violence can spoil all of our interpersonal relationships that we have the law or interdiction "Thou shalt not kill." Violence causes a short circuit and the voice of conscience becomes the verdict of a court. We need to take the reverse path, from interdiction-verdict to the injunction to live well.

Third challenge. The otherness of the conscience can be found in the Freudian superego, the internalization of the ancestral voice. The otherness in the heart of the conscience is a form of the passivity of the self. The question is, if there is a *trace* of the other in conscience, is that other ancestral, or God, or "an empty place"? Ricoeur's ontological essay concludes, "With this aporia of the Other, philosophical discourse comes to an end"(355).

But, of course, philosophical discourse does not come to an end, neither for Paul Ricoeur nor for us. We have taken but the first step in a careful reading of the text, lent a sympathetic ear to the arguments, reached a thorough understanding of the issues and the debates. Now, it is our time to respond, to criticize, to propose, to argue, and, finally, to advance our philosophical understanding of "oneself as another."

We can take *Oneself as Another,* the last, the most carefully constructed, and most tightly argued of Ricoeur's books, as the very model of his philosophical style. After a lifetime as a professor of philosophy, he always gives credit to other authors, and honors them by a careful and sympathetic reading of their arguments. He rejects completely any kind of foundationalism, such as those of Descartes or Husserl; but he equally rejects the nihilism and skepticism of Nietzsche. Where others see only dichotomies, Ricoeur sees dialectics. But, his dialectics never result in a "lazy eclecticism," or mere combination of elements from both poles, but rather in a "reading through" from one pole to the other in order to show their interdependence. His dialectical analyses do not result in a Hegelian "third term" which surpasses the dialectical poles and renders them useless. His "third term," such as "practical wisdom," can only be undertood at the very heart of the dialectic and as completely implying both poles of the dialectic. This is a constant and essential element in his philosophical method.

Oneself as Another is not only an excellent example of Ricoeur's philosophical style, but it clearly exemplifies and continues his lifelong interest in human action and suffering. He himself has characterized his work as a "philosophical anthropology." His work is at the crossroads between "words and deeds," or a "semantics of action and desire." it is in this sense that his last book recapitulates and refines his central philosophical concerns.

· 4 ·

INTERVIEWS

Chatenay-Malabry, June 19, 1982

*T*HIS INTERVIEW *with Paul Ricoeur was taped at his house in Chatenay-Malabry, France, on June 19, 1982. I have edited the transcript of the tape to make it more readable. The interview was originally made for my students in a course on contemporary hermeneutics. (The first three interviews in this chapter were conducted in English; the fourth was done in French. The translation from the French is mine.)*

REAGAN: Paul, you use the term "hermeneutics" to describe the kind of philosophy you have been practicing since 1960. Would you give us a brief account of what you mean by hermeneutics?

RICOEUR: I think that we must keep in mind that the word "hermeneutics" expresses a task, the task of interpreting. Therefore, we must never separate our notion of hermeneutics from the term "interpretation." It's a kind of learned word for the task of interpretation. I would like to characterize it by some negative traits and also some more positive ones. Negatively, I would say it is some general mistrust concerning the claim of any philosophy to reestablish the primacy of intuition, immediacy, as though we could have before us in our minds the pure presence of what is. In negative terms, hermeneutics is a kind of mourning of the immediate, and the recognition that we have only an indirect relationship to what is; we shall discuss whether we have to keep the expression "what is." But, at any rate, the first application of the term "hermeneutics" is that we have to give up the project of intuitionist philosophy either in the tradition of Platonism, Neo-Platonism, or its modern equivalents. Some aspects of the phenomenology we shall discuss have this intuitionist claim in the tradition of Descartes—as though we could be without distance to ourselves.

The positive counterpart of this negative description, this negative concession, is that we have to integrate a kind of mediated relation through signs—linguistic signs or cultural institutions—which Cassirer called the system of symbols, including art or science and religious symbols. But, we move among signs which stand for something, and therefore this will bring me to the third trait of hermeneutics. It is to develop the requirement of any signative system as standing-for and thus to reconstruct the meditations implied in this "standing-for." Literally it is the sense of the substitutive function of the sign that it refer through its own specific intentionality. Therefore, I should say that the word hermeneutics will be the task of the explication of all the symbolic systems which relate us indirectly to reality, whatever this reality may be. And this will be, I suppose, one of the stakes, that is, one of the ontological premises.

REAGAN: Well, as you know, the term "hermeneutics" is quite in vogue now. I am wondering if you would distinguish your view from that of Dilthey, and then perhaps of two contemporaries, Gadamer and Habermas. What are some of the main points where you differ from them?

RICOEUR: I would like first to underline my debt to them. As deep as may be the gaps and differences between what I am attempting to do and what Dilthey did, I think that at least there are in common some basic propositions. First, that we move among readings. So I think that this is something decisive when Dilthey said that in the sciences of nature, this *Naturwissenschaften,* we have to do with facts. With human beings, we have to do with signs—reading. Secondly, we have a debt to the later Dilthey which has been too often overlooked for the sake of his first work where he was putting the emphasis mainly on psychology, that is, where hermeneutics was understood as the capacity of reading, so to speak, other minds through their expressions. But the later Dilthey laid the stress on two complementary and, in a sense corrective, problems. The first is that we must deal with the systematic organization of signs, what he called *Zusammenhange* and which we might translate as "connections or coherent wholes." This implies a holistic approach to the system of signs. It is in the sense that science constitutes organized wholes that we see already in Dilthey the surmise of what we call today the "textual," the texture of organization. The second is his insistence on the role of writing as a fixation of these connections, these interconnected signs. Thanks to this fixation, the fact that they become institutions, monuments of culture independent from their authors, he has prefigured a theme which is now presupposed by structural analysis, that is, that texts have a destiny of their own distinct from the intentions of their authors.

In one of his important essays, "The Origin of Hermeneutics" (of which there is a very good English translation), he says that the difference between comprehension (*Verstehen*) and interpretation (*auslegung*) lies precisely in this intermediary role of fixation and all the equivalents of writing which have the same purpose and the same effect. That is, they provided to the text a fate, a destiny of its own. Therefore, the text is open to interpretation beyond any psychological reconstruction of the intention of the author. So I am more dependent on this tradition of the later Dilthey than on the first Dilthey who opposed *Naturwissenschaften* and *Geisteswissenschaften*.

There are also lateral reasons for not following the first Dilthey. We are now no longer sure about this deep gap between the so-called science of the spirit and the so-called science of nature. The notion of fact in the natural sciences is strongly put in doubt and criticized. There is also interpretation in the field of the natural sciences. On the other hand, there are also explanatory moments within the science of the spirit which will not allow us to put a strong distinction between nature and spirit. There is also some exchange in the sense that there is more interpretation in the natural sciences than Dilthey thought and there is a place for explanation in the sciences of the text. So therefore, for my part, I should say that the dialectic between explanation and understanding no longer coincides with the difference between natural and human. Even within the boundaries of the human sciences, the dialectic of explanation and understanding is an inner dialectic and it is constitutive of interpretation.

REAGAN: Given that there are quite a lot of similarities between your view of hermeneutics and, say, Gadamer's, what would you point out as being the main difference or distinction?

RICOEUR: I try to—I dare not say to mediate between Gadamer and Habermas: they don't need me for doing that—but I try to take a kind of equal distance to both because I have a debt to both and also I try to understand one through the other. I will give an example of that. Gadamer is mainly, I should say, a man of tradition. As one of his main disputes with Heidegger, he never emphasizes the so-called destruction of ontology. He is more aware of and more eager to preserve the continuity of tradition because he has a fundamental concept—one I think is very important—that of the "classic." For him there is an authority in classics because he considers that there are great texts of humanity which are, so to say, decontextualized by their very capacity for surviving all the cultural revolutions and which are always able to be recontextualized in new cultural situations—and in a sense which preserves a kind of authority. So it is this authoritative character of the traditional texts as classic which puts the task of interpretation under the control of the authority of the texts. I think that this notion of authoritative goes beyond that of authorial. It is not the authority of the author but the authority of the text itself.

Habermas is an heir of the post-Marxist tradition, mainly of the Frankfurt school. He is very suspicious of this concept of authority since all his concern, especially in the middle stage of his development, was to open the field of what he called emancipatory works. Therefore, the opposition of emancipation to authority is, I think, a key to the opposition between them. This did not prevent Habermas from paying his own tribute to Gadamer, in that he broke with positivism and with the instrumentalist concept of reason. Habermas took hermeneutics as a transition from one function of reason, which is to dominate, to organize, and finally, to rule, to its other function, which is to liberate, by opening a field of discussion which he considered as his utopian stage, without boundaries or constraints. So therefore, it is in between these two interpretations of hermeneutics that I try to find my own place.

REAGAN: You describe your view as hermeneutic phenomenology. But isn't that a contradiction since phenomenology describes what appears and hermeneutics is the search for the hidden?

RICOEUR: Maybe there is something deceptive in this too-sharp an opposition between what appears and what is hidden. On the one hand, if you look at the method of phenomenology, what appears has to be discovered, in the sense that it is a very long preparatory procedure for Husserl to get to the given. In a sense we could say that the given is not at hand. What about the famous problem of "bracketing," of putting out of work, the objective approach and, therefore, to get to the region of consciousness and meaning? It is a very hard and long detour. So in a sense the given is the last region to which we get access. On the other hand, at least at the beginning of *Being and Time*, Heidegger kept repeating that what is the closest is precisely what is hidden. So, we must not take the term "hidden" in a kind of hermetic sense, confused with the hermeneutic sense. It does not mean that there is a kind of hidden as though we had to open a sealed text in the tradition of occultism. On the contrary, it is what is under the light of the sun which is hidden because it has been covered by some accretion of culture or science whose appearance we get by bracketing objectivity, to use Husserl's terms. In Heidegger, we have a kind of parallel concept, "forgetfulness." It is not so much that a layer covers the hidden, but, on the contrary, that it is our being-in-the-world, to use the vocabulary, that has been forgotten. So the fight against oblivion is, in a sense, more important than the fight against the adjunction of science, technology, and so on.

REAGAN: So you would say this is really not a true opposition at all?

RICOEUR: It is not a true opposition. There is a tension between the two poles of what appears and what is hidden and what appears is precisely what was hidden. The task is to make it appear.

REAGAN: It is clear in your own case that you arrived at hermeneutics through and after phenomenology, but what really is left of classical phenomenology? In short, does hermeneutics need phenomenology?

RICOEUR: I should like to forget for a while what is merely contingent in my personal itinerary, that is, the fact that I translated the *Ideen* of Husserl and that I was in charge of the Husserl Archive in Paris and also that there is a kind of personal commitment to phenomenology. But I will say that we cannot imagine modern hermeneutics—I mean by that post-Heideggerian hermeneutics—without the transition through phenomenology. It is more than a kind of personal problem. It is a structural connection in the history of modern thought that the kind of hermeneutics that we know, which is not that of Dilthey and still less that of Schleiermacher, had to be preceded by phenomenology. I offer two reasons: First, because whatever we may think about the idealistic interpretation of phenomenology of Husserl, it is to Husserl that we owe the opening of the field of the "meaningful." And, this is the necessary transition: *Being and Time* says that being is a phenomenology, a phenomenology of, let us say *Sorge* (care). But it is not a break; rather it is a broadening of the philosophy of intentionality. The second theme has been transposed or expanded beyond the limit of an idealistic version of phenomenology. I should say that hermeneutics, the Heideggerian and post-Heideggerian hermeneutics, is the liberation of phenomenology from a certain limitation owed to the allegiance to idealism. It is finally what remains neo-Kantian. I would say that with respect to Husserl the broadening of phenomenology through hermeneutics is also a kind of liberation of phenomenology. This is more or less in the sense that the given is the hidden and the hidden is the given. There is a continuous development from the notion of intentionality to that of being-in-the-world. In a sense, Husserl remained within the framework of a theory of knowledge with the relation of subject/object. It is this relationship, subject/object, which has been overcome by the many ways in which we are inserted in a world and also committed to a concerned participation and belonging to the world. And, I think it would be wrong to say that this is a realism opposed to an idealism, because realism was also trapped in the subject/object relationship and therefore was the opposite of idealism, but only within that relationship.

REAGAN: You frequently speak of a conflict of interpretations—in fact, you have a book by that name. What is the criterion or criteria for choosing amongst conflicting interpretations, say of a text?

RICOEUR: I think it is important that your question is raised within the framework of the concept of the text. Therefore, the limits of the question imply also the limitation of the answer. If we stay within the limit of a text, I should confess that there are no sure criteria for choosing among the conflicting interpretations. If we are not allowed to say anything that we want about a text, there is a kind of space of possibility between the text having just one meaning and just any meaning. There is always a range of plausible meanings, and therefore the question of criteria belongs to a certain kind of interpretation itself, that is to say, to a coming to an agreement between arguments. So it presupposes a certain model of rationality where universality, verification, and so on are compelling.

Maybe the conflict of interpretation implies, also includes, what we mean by criteria and what is at stake with the concept of criteria. For example, if we consider the tradition of suspicion—what I called in the past "the hermeneutics of suspicion"—this is precisely what is at stake. If you take Nietzsche, Freud, and maybe also Marx—in spite of the fact that Marx finally belongs more to the tradition of rationalism than Freud and Nietzsche—they put in question the very idea of criteria, that is, of solving the problem by a good criteriology. This is why the conflict is so embarrassing, so puzzling, because it includes the rules of the game which did not belong to the conflict itself. This is why we cannot escape the seriousness of conflicts of interpretation, but also why we must try to find a way out through a strategy which keeps together the two poles.

We can take as an example what I tried to do with Freud. I tried to go as far as possible along the line of suspicion, for which all symbolic thought would be an extension of fancy and yes, phantasy. And, it is to this extent that we carry the burden of this possibility, or precisely the seriousness with which we take the reduction of all figures of authority—political, ethical, religious—as an expansion of Oedipal conflict. This is an example, and it is not by excluding this possibility, but, on the contrary, by going as far as possible, accompanying it to its extreme consequences, that we may see the emergence of a displacement (to use the vocabulary of Lacan) from what he called imagination to what he called symbolic. So, therefore, we say that we have to disentangle the one contrary from the other. But, in order to complete, or to give the complement to the answer, we must not forget that everything is not a text.

So, the first part of my answer was to say, let us take for granted the delineation of the question itself concerning texts, and, so long as there are texts, maybe that the level of the textual does not allow more than a certain plausibility of several interpretations which have, in a sense, an equal right. But, not everything is a text in the sense that texts themselves are the product of a culture and have not only an origin, a birth, but also implications and effects from, and in, life and human action. Here we border on the problem of ethics and politics and then you have a different kind of problem which is maybe no longer hermeneutical, in the sense that it is not within interpretation ruled by reading.

There may be ethical choices that we make or we have made and we put them in question in the proper way. But as you said in a previous conversation, it is impossible to put everything in question at the same time. No discussion would be possible if we did not take for granted something else. So therefore, there are always in the background of every hermeneutical discussion some commitments somewhere, which are not put in question during the time of the discussion. We may proceed to a kind of "questioning back" of this past position. But then something else is taken for granted. So, in a sense, not everything is under our control in the discussion, as though we were in a shop choosing between two neckties. Not all of the elements of the choice are before us and we are not in the position of indifference between possibilities. We have already chosen for something by the very fact that we are committed to something when we put in question something else. So here we are beyond the criteriology, not only within the text but outside the text as well.

REAGAN: This discussion leads right into the next question. In the *Rule of Metaphor* and in your latest work, *Time and Narrative*, you speak of the power of metaphors and narratives to redescribe the world. This implies first of all a power of description. But if we are going to talk about descriptions of something, of the world, how do we avoid the "mirror of nature" problem on which Richard Rorty has recently written?

RICOEUR: I must say that I am not so happy with this expression, "redescribe the world," and what I am now doing with time and narrative would precisely avoid this expression. I am reminded of the origin of this expression which is not, I should say, appropriate to what I was doing in *The Rule of Metaphor*. It is a transposition from the field of the theory of models. I borrowed the expression from people like Mary Hesse and Max Black because they start from a situation where something has been already decided in terms of a description. Then the help that I was expecting from their model is that the same thing happens with poetic language. There is already a use of language which is literal meaning. We cannot imagine a language which would be poetic through and through. But it is always against the background of ordinary language, of conventional meanings, that there is a breakthrough of metaphorical language. So to transfer from a theory of models to a theory of metaphor the concept of description and redescription does not mean that I am committed to a representational philosophy of description. It means only that, exactly as we said, it is impossible to put in question everything in a discussion without having a background.

In the same way, when we enter into the problematic either of metaphor or narrative, there is already a background. There is, in the case of narrative, an experience of action, of what a human action is, and how it has been already recounted by previous stories, and then we retell in a new way what has been told already in a certain way. For example, when the historian starts again with a new interpretation of the French Revolution, we say that he redescribes it in the sense that he starts from a state of the problem where there is a confusion between a very strict concept of description as opposed to prescription, and so on. So it belongs to the very specific vocabulary of linguistic philosophy or, more precisely, analytical philosophy. In a broader sense, we can say, following Nelson Goodman in this case, that there are many renderings of our relation to a world; when the painter, for example, tries to give a new rendering of a landscape, there is another relationship to this landscape which is not shattered by the fact that he fights with the previous tradition in painting. For, he goes on with a pragmatic relation to the world with also a perceptual relationship to the world. It is in this sense what we may say that there is a background of description for any new attempt to redescribe something. But once more, I think that it is maybe after the book of Rorty that we may have more important reasons to drop the confusion of description, if it is true that the word "description" commits us to a theory of representation as knowing the world. I don't see why the background of description which provides for a new rendering of the world should be representation in that sense. As for me, my own approach to the problem of metaphor and narrative is to say that there is a reshaping of our way of looking at things which, in a sense, is no longer description, and surely no longer representational in the sense of Rorty.

It is a creative referentiality. So the problem of what could be a creative reference to reality is raised and we must ask, what is the fate of the concept of reality when it is delivered from the yoke of the representational tradition?

REAGAN: Well, of course, you frequently talk of the world of the text or in some places the world which the text creates which is a possible world for me. What is the relation between this world and the real world we live in? In other words, what is the difference between narratives or interpretations which claim to be history and those which only claim to represent fictional or possible worlds?

RICOEUR: I suggest that this is a very complex question because, first of all, there is this notion of "world." I keep saying that what is ultimately important in the text and in the work of art in general is not the object which it depicts but the world that it generates. This is to say there is a horizon of experience which is not exhausted by the things and people and so on which are depicted or represented in one way or the other. This is the sort of notion that the world is a very irreducible concept. It means what is inexhaustible in terms of object in a situation. So it is always a background. It means that in each situation there is something which is not chosen; but with the closure of the situation there is the openness of a certain angle of vision. Therefore, in the notion of angle of vision there is both the strict limitation of origin of this angle of vision, but at the same time openness on something which is not exhausted by the foreground, the second ground, and so on. There is a background which is inexhaustible and then which can be joined with the horizon of another onlooker. This is the problem specific to Gadamer—what he called "fusion of horizons," as the point of encounter of several visions of the world.

The second part of my answer would concern the fact that we are speaking of two worlds, one of which is fictional because it is projected by the work. It is the world of the work—or, the work's world. But as a reader, I belong to two worlds, the fictional world displayed by the work and the one in which I live, in the sense that I display my action so that the actual world is the world of a praxis. That leads me to say that reading is not an innocent, or still less an uninteresting, act. It is the decisive intersection between the world of the work and the world of actual praxis because it is the act through which there is a permanent transfer from the fictional world to the real world.

Here, I fight against the claim that texts constitute by themselves a world or a closed world. It is only by methodological decision that we say that the world of literature, let us say, constitutes a world of its own. It is only in libraries that texts are closed on themselves—and even then only when nobody reads them. So then, we have a closed world of texts in a library, but literature is not a big library. It is by the act of reading that I follow a certain trajectory, a trajectory of meaning of the text. Then I reenact in a certain sense the dynamic course of the text and I prolong this dynamic beyond the text itself. In other words, the distinction between the inside and the outside of the text is created by a methodological decision, that of considering texts only as closed on themselves. I think that it is a task of hermeneutics to reopen this closure and to reinsert the world of literature between what precedes it, let us say a kind of naive experience, and what succeeds it, that is to say, a learned experience. So, in a sense, the act of reading has this wonderful quality of interpolating the world of literature between the stage of unlearned experience to a stage of learned experience and praxis. It is in this sense that I speak of the hermeneutical arch through which the work of art is a mediation between man and the world, between man and another man, and between man and himself. So it is a mediating stage in a process of communication, man and man; referentiality, or man and the world; but also self-understanding, man and himself.

REAGAN: This leads us to my last question: what is the relation between hermeneutics as you have described it and philosophy conceived in its traditional sense? Is hermeneutics the whole of philosophy, or one method amongst others, or one branch of philosophy? How do you see the relationship between hermeneutics and philosophy?

RICOEUR: I am very puzzled by the question, and I must say that I have no good reason to be, because I should say that philosophy is defined by the kind of questions that are raised. There was philosophy because Parmenides raised the problem of being, non-being, and so forth. So the field of the questions raised by philosophers constitutes philosophy. There is philosophy because Descartes raised the problem of the first truth, because Kant raised the problem of the synthetic a priori judgment. So, therefore, hermeneutics is limited in the sense that it does not have the key of the origin of questions and the capacity of renewing the questions. In that sense it would be foolish and merely an arrogant claim to say that now philosophy can be only hermeneutical. There is a modesty in the answer which must be appropriate to the greatness of the philosophical tradition. And one of your suggestions is precisely to raise the problem of the relationship between hermeneutics and ethics and politics.

I should say that hermeneutics has both an inclusive and an exclusive sense. Or, a relation of inclusion and a relation of exclusion both. There is a relation of inclusion to the extent that we just said a moment ago that interpretation is not limited to the boundary of the text. As soon as we raise the problem of application or appropriation, or whatever may be the word, then we go out of the world of texts and to the field of life and action. And, then we are confronted by ethical questions and political questions. So in that sense, a hermeneutics, I should not say implies, but calls for, a development of a different kind ruled by new problems. And, why is it unable to include ethics and politics at a time when it requires it? This is because, I think, that there is this limitation by the concept of text. We return to that. The text, the notion of text has a broad scope but should not be equated to everything. So there is a kind of inner limitation to hermeneutics as an approach to the whole field of philosophy, including ethics and politics. This is simply the hermeneutical limitation to what is text. Even if we extend the notion of text beyond writing, nevertheless, it is this notion of fixation in documents which have reading as their counterpart. It is important for a discipline to know its own limits. If it identifies itself with the whole field of possible questions, it becomes meaningless.

REAGAN: Thanks, Paul.

Chicago, October 26, 1988

REAGAN: The last recorded interview we did was in June of 1982 at your house in Chatenay-Malabry. Since then, you have written a three-volume work, *Time and Narrative*. In addition, you have published your collection, *Du Texte à l'action*, in France, and finally, you have given the Gifford Lectures in Edinburgh, Scotland. So, I would like to ask you a few questions about each of these books you have done since our last interview. *Time and Narrative* is a magisterial work. But it seems to me it is a very difficult book for your readers since very few of us know both Anglo-American and French philosophical and literary traditions. Personally, I found volume 2 especially difficult. More so than 1 and 3. Maybe because I have been reading in philosophy rather than in literary theory. So I would like to know how the work has been received in France and in the U.S., and your general impression of it looking back now several years after the last volume was published.

RICOEUR: As concerns the reception of the work, I must say that it has been well received in France, because the philosophical scene has changed so much since not only the death of Merleau-Ponty in the early 1960s, but also the deaths of Michel Foucault and Jacques Lacan. Also, there is less arrogance among the figures of philosophy. It is more scattered. Maybe it lacks leading figures. We have, on the one hand, a development of quasi Anglo-American philosophy in the sense of analytical philosophy. There is the influence of the German school of Frankfurt and a new role of political philosophy in a more rationalistic sense. And, there is a strong revival in Hegelian, Nietzschean, and Heideggerian studies. So the French scene is very fragmented. People of my age, like Levinas, of the same generation, we have the impression of having survived so many changes that our own identity seems to be threatened by these rapid changes in the landscape. For example, structuralism more or less faded and existentialism belongs completely to the past. After working for thirty or forty years, it is difficult to speak about one's own identity in this crisis. But I think that I kept a certain line of thought. On the other hand, I try to do my best to borrow what could be accommodated to my own way of thinking. So there is this kind of screening between those with whom I have nothing to do and those who can nourish my own thinking. This is the way I could keep my own line and at the same time respond to the change of landscape.

REAGAN: How would you say that *Time and Narrative* has been received in the United States?

RICOEUR: I think it is too early to tell because it is too big a work. It is addressed to several publics and not each one has responded. I have the impression that there is a kind of hesitation in face of this work. I don't know whether I am right or not. I have not read the reviews except the harsh attack in the *TLS* by a critic belonging to the deconstructionist school. I have an impression of a kind of polite reception. I don't know; maybe it is too early.

REAGAN: It could be, since the third volume has only been published in English during the last year.

RICOEUR: Yes, and because the third one is difficult since it joins philosophy—

a review of the main theories of temporality—and historiography, the theory of historic writing, and literary criticism. If I may say something about these three aspects, to which correspond three different audiences, I would say, as concerns temporality, my claim is that the problem of time is loaded by antinomies, aporias, not because the philosophies we have about time as are not well conceived, but because the problem of time generates antinomies. I give only one example: When we speak of the present, we have two readings, if I may say so, of the present. On the one hand, we may say it is only a kind of point—point-like instant—in the flow of changing things. This would be the external approach to the problem of time as a cosmological problem. This is one dimension of temporality, that it is the inner structure of reality besides me—an external reality. But on the other hand, I may speak of the present as opposed to the past and the future, in the sense that I opposed the intuitive grasp of the presence of things to the memories of past events or to the expectation of future events. So I have a notion of the present not as a point which would slip right through half-lines, but to the contrary, a gathering moment where expectation, memory, and present experience coincide. And so, whereas the cosmological instant is a kind of empty place—it is a caesura, a gap between two halves—the present, on the contrary, is a rich resource. It is a living moment; the present is now. I now live in this living present; there is concentration, a sort of shortcut, of expectations and memories. So the richness of the present may be opposed to the wholeness of the pure, point-like cosmological present. And my claim is that we have no way of overcoming this gap between the two approaches to time.

I try to show that in each period of the history of the problem this disparity, this polarity, kept recurring. I try to show that for ancient philosophy you have the approach by Aristotle which belongs to physics, but you have also the approach by Augustine which belongs to psychology. So we have the living present opposed to the physical instant. But in the modern age, you have the dispute about time between Clarke and Leibniz. We opposed a physical approach to a more mental approach to time. And, now we have the more subjectivist approach to time of Husserl. In physics there is a discussion about Newtonian time and microphysics in the quantum theory. There is no bringing together of these halves of the problem. This is my first claim: There is a kind of ultimate aporia in the constitution—the grasping—of time.

My second claim is that in narration—the art of telling—either in history or in fiction, you have not a solution in the speculative sense, but a response to the aporia. The structure of my third volume, which brings together the parts of the two first volumes, is based on this connection between the aporicity of temporal experience and the creative answer—what I call the "poetics" in a broad sense of the word poetics, the *poein*, the creative answer of narrativity. And so, the whole work thickens up—there is a leading thread between the aporicity of the time-experience and the creative answer of the act of narrating.

I attach a strong philosophical claim to the act of telling which is not merely entertainment but which has a philosophical responsibility. By the very act of telling we provide a certain structure to our experience. And, within those structures, we connect the physical and the mental. Most telling is about human action—what people did or suffered, either in the real world, this historical world, or in the imagined world, the fictional world of literature. But it has to do with people who do something in a world. Therefore, their actions connect the physical and the mental sides of time. I try to show that time which is construed by the act of narrative is a kind of third time in comparison with the physical or cosmological on the one hand, and the mental or psychical or phenomenological time on the other hand. So it is this bridge between these two parts of the philosophy of time. I try to show that the very act of telling is a kind of response to the aporia—not a solution, but a response.

REAGAN: In most of your books, you end with a summary of what questions you have been able to resolve and which ones have been left open to be resolved in your next book. I think that in *Freedom and Nature* and up through *Freud and Philosophy* it is quite clear that there is a direction. *Time and Narrative* ends somewhat modestly; it doesn't chart out what the next step will be. Maybe you think you have said as much as you possibly can on the problem of time and narrative and now you want to move off to something that is not related.

RICOEUR: Well, there is the sense of a direction, at least one direction which I see is now my task. I try to say that by telling a story we construct the identity not only of the characters of the story but the character of the reader. This leads me to the problem of narrative identity. And so, my present work, the Gifford Lectures, is addressed to the problem of selfhood. I try to show that the unity of a life is the unity of a told story. I address myself to a problem which is widely discussed in present Anglo-American philosophy, the problem of personal identity. You have very important works—this problem was raised in the English-speaking world first by Locke in his philosophy of the understanding. The response of Hume was that "You are looking for a subject; I don't find it." It is only a "bundle of impressions"—you know the famous expression. It kept recurring with Kant, who searched for the identity of the "I think." It was also the topic of Nietzsche, mainly in his last works, such as the *Will to Power* where he denies there is anything like the unity and identity of a subject.

So I thought that my previous work on time and narrative could provide me with a better approach to identity. I submit this hypothesis to you: The word "identity" itself is a very polemic term because we mean two different things by the word. First, *sameness;* as when I say that between a young plant and a full-grown tree there is an identity of structure. We know now that there is a kind of genetic structure of beings which remains the same. But there may be a second reading of the term "identity" which we have, for example, in the experience of responsibility. I don't claim to be the same, but I impose on myself the duty to be faithful to my word. This will to keep one's word implies a quite different sense of identity. Not as sameness, but as "*ipséité.*" This comes from the Latin word, *ipse.* Even if I have changed, I am bound by my promise. The subject, bound by its own promise, comprises a sense of identity which is quite different than the identity of sameness of structure. Sameness of structure is a kind of denial of time. In spite of time, the same structure prevails.

So, this way of preserving the identity of a structure through time is quite different from the route along which, by constructing the story of our life, we elaborate an identity which is completely a narrative kind. And it is this narrative identity which is the basis for an ethical life. I took the example of the promise because it is typical of the way in which I bind myself. So I try to connect the ethical problem of responsibility to the narrative structure of the person, of the human.

REAGAN: I have read two versions of the Gifford Lectures, and, as you told me last night, you plan to finish them up and publish them in the spring. I found the last two chapters on morality and politics especially interesting. You put "violence" at the origin of politics and morality and you look at it from the point of view of the victim rather than the point of view of the agent. This, to me, is a rather novel way of approaching the problems of ethics and of politics.

RICOEUR: Yes, this is linked to a broader concern of mine which is not completely satisfied by my Gifford Lectures; it is the place of suffering in human experience. I keep saying that in stories, in history, in narrative of all kinds we have to do with acting and suffering people. In fact, all my work is about acting, but not about suffering. I try to cast at least a glance in that direction through ethics because it is an access to the problems of ethics by saying that by my action I entertain a process of victimization which keeps going on through history. In action, there is a basic asymmetry, because agents have not only agents in front of them but patients. Or, as Alan Gewirth says, "recipients of my actions." The source of the ethical problem is that we have to redress this asymmetrical relationship of the agent and the patient. The whole problem of justice finds its starting point here because justice is concerned with the kinds of institutions or structured action which attempt to redress this asymmetry by saying that there is a basic equality between men. In fact, this equality is permanently denied by the fact that someone exerts power over someone else.

When I say that this is a good approach to the ethical problem, I could say that a second reading of Kant would lead in the same direction. When he says in the second formulation of the categorical imperative that we must treat others not only as means, but also as ends in themselves, it implies the first move is to treat the other as a means. That is to say—a polite way to say— oppression, that is, extortion, or obedience, a way to make the other into a tool. To use another access to the same problem, Habermas says that we have to make communicative rationality prevail over instrumental rationality. But what is instrumental rationality if not the way in which we use strategic action to impose the will of someone on the will of someone else? This relationship between action and passion, or agent and patient, I take as the threshold of the moral problem.

I must say that in my previous work there is very little about ethics and politics. It is this speculative problem of action and passion but also the prob- lem of victimization—the whole story of this cruel century, the twentieth century—and all of the suffering imposed on the Third World by the rich, affluent countries, by colonialism. There is a history of victims that keeps accompanying or reduplicating the history of the victors. But the history I try to revive has a strong ethical debt to the victims.

REAGAN: Do you foresee a systematic book on ethics or politics?

RICOEUR: The situation in which I am now is rather fuzzy because, on the one hand, I am more or less finished with the Gifford Lectures. First, because I gave the Gifford Lectures two and a half years ago. So they exist in that way. But I keep amplifying them. I don't know whether what I am now doing on the problem of justice as an ethical, political, and juridical problem should be added to that or whether I should keep that for a further study. At the end of *Time and Narrative*, it was not easy to see where I could go further. But I make a suggestion which has nothing to do with what you just said—or only an indirect connection—because I suggest that narration is not the only way to get access to the problem of time. This is one of the conclusions of the book which is a kind of redirection when I say that the strict correlation between temporality and narrativity in a sense explodes because I concede that narrati- vity does not take hold of time. This is the ultimate meaning of Proust's work; we never recover time.

There is a lyrical—I should say elegiac—aspect of time which is not in- cluded in the heroic side of narrative which claims to take hold of temporality by imposing a structure. I could say that *Time and Narrative* fails, but exactly as I say that we respond to the aporia of temporality through the creativity of narrative, we could say that this attempt itself is aporetic. There is an aporia of the response because the narrative is not capable of overcoming all the aporias of temporality. We have other accesses to temporality besides narration. Maybe a reflection or meditation on the creative aspects we have in aesthetics, in morality and in politics, also in the myths of creation—in what we call the sense of the gift—would provide a quite different approach to suffering and evil than narrativity.

REAGAN: Do you see a direct connection between the hermeneutics of texts and the understanding of moral and political obligations?

RICOEUR: The problem of rights and obligations is not completely included within the problem of texts, but, nevertheless, we may say they have a textual dimension. Let us take for example the problem of law, written law. We learn from history that it is when the laws are written that there is really justice, when the judgment of the tribunals and the courts are independent of the whims of the judge. So you have this textual dimension of the written law. Even in the common law, the British and American common law, you have precedents. The judgments are in accordance with precedents but also the discretion of the judge, who has to construct a new rule which could solve the hard cases without betraying the precedents. So you have a hermeneutics which is similar to the hermeneutics of the sacred texts or the hermeneutics of literary texts. This was very well seen by Betti, one of the theoreticians of hermeneutics, who said that there are three branches of hermeneutics: hermeneutics of sacred texts, hermeneutics of profane texts, and juridical hermeneutics.

The interpretation of texts and precedents and the invention of a new solution for the so-called "hard" cases provide us with a very interesting approach to the problem of generating new meanings. My own work, both in *The Rule of Metaphor* and my book on narrative, is about the creative aspects of language. But we have this creative process going on in the domain of law. I have just started reading in the recent English literature about the problem of justice. But I don't know whether it will become a book or just a private exercise.

REAGAN: The colloquium at Cérisy broke up in a bit of a hurry on the last day. What were your impressions of your ten days there, the quality of the papers, and the level of the discussion?

RICOEUR: I was grateful for this opportunity to spend ten or eleven days with my colleagues and friends. They behaved neither as disciples nor as enemies, foes, but as collaborators trying to work with me—not about my work, but about the problems which prompted me to write these books. So the whole colloquium was about the problems on which I worked for more than thirty years. Therefore, there was an equality among all the speakers and me. You,

Charles, were one of the most helpful contributors to this research. Second, I should like to emphasize plurality not only of philosophical schools, but of epistemological approaches, since there were people who were trained in linguistics, or theory of language, or biblical exegesis, others in psychoanalysis, others in historiography, yet others in metaphysics. So the range was huge and corresponded broadly to the many departments of my own interests. Third, there was an international character to this gathering, since over half of the members were non-French. Some were from Australia, northern Europe, American, Canada, Scandinavia. For me it was a kind of reward, with people coming from so many quarters, not only in terms of geography, but of competencies and interests. To summarize, it was a very happy time for me.

REAGAN: According to Jean Greisch and others, there was an atmosphere that was more collegial and friendly than at some other colloquia.

RICOEUR: Yes, because this kind of colloquium may succumb to three different kinds of diseases: Either boredom because they become repetitious very early—this was not the case because there were so many different approaches. Or hostility—people come to "kill" the guest or the other participants. Or obedience—even a kind of submission of disciples to the master. I think we escaped all of these pitfalls. Is this your impression?

REAGAN: Yes, I thought it went very well, and I was surprised when Jean Greisch told me they don't always go so smoothly.

RICOEUR: I think this was one of the most gratifying experiences of my life.

REAGAN: Well, thank you very much, Paul. I am at the end of my questions.

RICOEUR: I was obscure and cryptic in my answers concerning what I am now working on because I am caught in this difficulty—closing the workshop of the Gifford Lectures. I have to make a drastic decision in the following weeks.

Chicago, May 17, 1990

REAGAN: Paul, this is the third of a series of interviews we have done together. The first one was in Chatenay-Malabry in June 1982. We spoke about your work on Freud, your work on metaphor, and your then-recent work on hermeneutics leading up to *Time and Narrative*. The second interview took place in Chicago in October 1988. In that interview, we talked mostly about the three volumes of *Time and Narrative* and the work you were then doing on revising the Gifford Lectures. In this interview, I would like to concentrate on three events which have occurred since that interview: First, the publication of *Du texte à l'action*. Second, the international colloquium at Cérisy-la-salle dedicated to your work; you were there and heard all of the papers and then gave the final paper. Finally, I would like to talk about your latest book, *Soi-*

même comme un autre, which, in the main, came out of the Gifford Lectures. Perhaps we could take these three themes one at a time.

RICOEUR: Thank you, Charles. You remember these interviews better than I do. With respect to my book, *Du texte à l'action*, it is the third volume of my essays published during a thirty-year period. *History and Truth* contains my essays on a variety of topics during the 1950s. *The Conflict of Interpretations* is a collection of my essays written during the 1960s, when I was interested in hermeneutics and Freud and problems in the philosophy of langauge. *Du texte à l'action* contains my essays written during the 1970s and 1980s. It is quite different from the other books because, first, there are very few footnotes and so it is more direct. There are few confrontations with other thinkers, so it is a more personal but also a less elaborated expression of the development of my thought. As I say in the preface, I do hermeneutics instead of justifying doing it. I do it directly so it is less defensive. Secondly, it expresses the move which I made during this ten last years from more specifically linguistic questions. If I extend linguistics from the theory of the text, written language, to the problem of action, in a sense, it comes full circle, since I started with *The Voluntary and the Involuntary*, which was already a kind of theory of action in a phenomenological mode. So I return to my starting point. But at the end of this long journey through the problem of the text, I keep seeing that human action is basically structured by symbols, laws, and so on. Therefore, as the symbols and laws are gathered and preserved and enhanced by writing, the move from text to action is a natural one. Also, they are linked, since I have always said that language has a referent outside of itself; action is one of these referents and, to a certain extent, the most important referent—how we deal with our environment, with other people, and so on. The world of action is the world of the reader of the text. This is the connection.

Second, the *décade* at Cérisy is a different kind of event since it was organized by two friends of mine, Richard Kearney and Jean Greisch, and the condition I had put to them to take part in this *décade* was that it would not be about me but about the problems with which I struggled. This is why among the fifteen or twenty essays which were read, only one-fourth may be said to be about me or were a presentation of my work. So it is more a confrontation of different points of view concerning the main problems which I covered during this thirty or forty years, precisely, language, psychoanalysis, and literature and metaphorical language, and all their related problems. And, I must say that this was for me a very rewarding experience because we spent ten days together without anybody leaving. So we made acquaintances and there was a kind of common language and nobody was aggressive and nobody wanted to embarrass me, but at the same time there was no subservient attitude. It was a free exchange and very very friendly. All of the contributions will be published next autumn. To some of them I owe much for a better understanding of what I intended to do and what I actually did and what I had not done but should have done. And, you were there and you may confirm my assessment of the *décade*.

As concerns the publication of *Soi-même comme un autre*, it is a long-delayed publication since the book was nearly finished one year ago and it is the last stage, I think, of the development of my theory of the subject, action, narrative, ethics, and so on. Of course, we shall speak of that in a moment. The present structure of the book is a bit different from the lectures which I gave at Edinburgh as the Gifford Lectures. At Edinburgh I gave ten lectures and the book covers only six of them plus some of the lectures which I added for reasons which I will explain in a moment. This book may be read in different ways because it is a multilayered book. I start with the linguistic level, then I move to the pragmatic level of action, and then to the problem of the personal identity with the narrative component of identity, and then to ethical problems, and finish with some excursions into the ontology of actions.

Then I move to a second question, since it is precisely about the change from the Gifford Lectures and you ask me what led me to add the section on ethics at the end. I should say for three reasons: First, I always felt that there was a missing link in my exploration of the anthropological problem, since I may say that my philosophy is a philosophical anthropology. So it needed this expansion in the ethical direction. Second, it is more tightly linked to the third problem of action, because I say somewhere that we have three ways of speaking about action. First, we can describe it, which is the function of the human sciences and also the Anglo-American so-called theory of action which I discuss at length. Second, action may be told, and then it is the function of narrative. Third, action may be prescribed, and therefore it is the connection between these three modes of discourse of action: describe, narrate, and prescribe. So it took a new unity of the concatenation of these three modes of language.

The third reason may be linked to the present state of the philosophical scene in Europe and perhaps in France: the need to reconstruct a political theory on a sound ethical basis. In a sense, this has always been my concern, the relationship between ethics and politics. But I wanted to deal with this not as a separate problem but as a part of this philosophical anthropology. This is why, in the section on ethics, there is one basic concept which makes the transition from ethics to politics, and that is the problem of justice. Then I discuss Rawls and Habermas. If I may open a parenthesis here, I would say that I

Les murs blancs, the Ricoeur residence in the Paris suburb of Catenay-Malabry, 1982.

The living room of the Ricoeurs' apartment at Les murs blancs, 1988.

Paul Ricoeur after he received an honorary doctorate at Ohio University in 1970.

Paul Ricoeur in 1982.

Ricoeur in a classroom at the University of Nanterre during a filming of an interview for an *Antenne 2* television program in 1991. The sign on the blackboard is the same as one put on a corridor wall by leftist students.

Paul Ricoeur at Préfailles in 1992.

Ricoeur in Chicago, 1990.

Ricoeur in 1995.

Ricoeur in his "serre."

Ricoeur in front of Monet's *Nymphéas* (1991).

have been reinforced in this conviction by what is happening right now in central Europe and especially in Czechoslovakia. I was a friend—I used to be and I am still—of Vaclav Havel, and his sense of politics as highly ethical reinforced me in this conviction that we need to build politics on the basis of ethics. It is not only the problem of civil rights and human rights, but the whole problem of justice as the fall of subjectivity when it has to do with a relation to another who is not in a face-to-face relationship with me. So it is the third person, if I dare say so, in action who is precisely the one who is the partner of any system of distribution. I added here the idea of Rawls that all society is a huge system of distribution, not only of roles in terms of patrimonies, but also the functions of position, of authority, of responsibility, and the others, and so on. Therefore, the classical problem of justice, coming from Aristotle in the *Nichomachean Ethics,* is the notion of proportional equality.

I think that it is the kernel of the problem, and this is why I am so much interested in the work of Rawls, which I interpret less as a Kantian philosophy but more as an Aristotelian philosophy, in the sense that the notion of proportional equality is the center of his system of distribution. So that explains the reason why I have introduced this section on ethics because, finally, it is the completion of the theory of action, from the description through narration to prescription.

And to add a word, I would say that that changes my own approach to the problem of narration, with which I dealt in *Time and Narrative* as a separate work and separate topic as related to time, and then tried to show how it is related to action because to narrate action is to provide paradigms for action. It is a paradigmatic function of narratives in relation to any projects or real horizon of actions. So the narrative here is taken as a transition between description and prescription. I tried to show how the narrative adds to the description of action and also provides models for prescriptives. I will speak of a narrative ethics in this sense. So I think that these sections on ethics are well-rooted in the whole project. I don't see them as parasitic, but as a necessary completion of the whole project.

REAGAN: Now, in the Gifford Lectures there were two lectures on religious narratives and the self.

RICOEUR: Yes, there were two lectures that I dropped. These two last ones were about the fate of the self in a religious context and I took as an example the biblical narratives of the call of the prophets. The prophet is summoned, then he loses his self, but his self is reinforced by the visions. I dropped that for two reasons. First, because I have a project more or less to gather up some of my essays on biblical hermeneutics and I think that will be the place for these essays. Second, I wanted to write a book which is truly philosophical without any religious affiliation. This is one of my claims on my work, that philosophy is autonomous activity and my own belonging to a religious tradition is based on and ruled by other criteria than those which I use in philosophy. So I wanted to confirm the complete independence of my work as a philosopher.

As I say in the preface, I cannot deny that there may be religious motivations in the very fact that I am interested in the self. But there is no self-interpreting motivation, although there may be some connection; but for the arguments, there is no recourse to any biblical argument in the whole work, even in the ethics section. I claim that ethics is not based on religion, but that religion is something other than a problem of duty. It is a problem of giving the gift, and so on like that. Love, for me, for example, does not belong to ethics; it belongs to a poetics of the will. So this is why I wanted to eliminate these lectures. And I have the agreement of Jean Greisch, precisely because he is himself a theologian and philosopher of reason. He does the same, and Levinas, too, in his philosophical books has no arguments from the Talmud. He writes his Talmudic studies separately. I am cautious not to mix things, to conflate, to alter our language.

REAGAN: What problems are you working on now?

RICOEUR: Unfortunately, I have no leading project because this last book left me with a kind of emptiness; it was a very difficult time, and I fell ill just after finishing the book. It is not by chance, I suppose, I had these heart problems last winter in Paris, after I gave the last portion of my book to my editor, François Wahl. It is very strange, kind of like women after the birth of a child. I am just recovering from that, thanks to teaching in Chicago.

I have three or four directions in mind, but it is very difficult to say which way I will go. I want to return to the problem of evil, but not as I did in the past, except in the small book called *Le Mal*, on the problem of suffering. I must say that I am more and more involved, for personal reasons or historical reasons, in the problem of suffering. It is also linked to the sense that something is missing, not only in my work but in philosophy at large, that is, an investigation of the field of feelings. I am struck by the fact that philosophers are always afraid to be accused of the affective fallacy. I have been reinforced in this conviction by the place that I give to literature, which is an exploration of feelings. Philosophical argument about feelings is so poor in treating the emotions, affects, and so on. There are connections with psychoanalysis, but also with moral feelings, which is a very rich field when you think of pride, of humility, of passion, of pity. We have only *actung*, Kant's sense of respect. It is not enough. So all this sphere of passivity, in fact, of human life, from sheer suffering to ethical feelings, is being ignored. I am sure that this needs much work.

First, I want to put in order my essays, which are very scattered, on biblical hermeneutics and biblical narratives. I have always been interested in the way which the Hebrew Bible and also the Gospel is organized in the narrative way, how it works, how the religious dimension is preserved, but exemplified by stories—the place of stories. But also I am interested in biblical hermeneutics because it connects many literary genres. For example, in the Hebrew Bible you have, of course, the narrative but also the legislative, the prescriptive, the prophetic, the eschatalogical, the hymnic, the sapiential. So there is intertextuality within the Bible. There is a new trend in biblical studies now to approach the Bible from a literary point of view because the historico-critical method has more or less exhausted its resources. To know who wrote what at what time is completely useless in understanding the text. So, the most interesting works written on the Bible are written not by exegetes but by literary critics, like Frank Kermode and Robert Alter. All of these people have written about Proust and Stendahl. I want to work in that direction. Maybe I will solve the problem of comparative religions, because I was always puzzled by this problem through my friendship and my work with Mircea Eliade. I want to be clear, but I need at least twenty or thirty years to do that. I am now recovering from this period of sadness—it was a kind of depression—and all the heart symptoms have more or less disappeared. Of course, I have good medication and all that. I feel ready to start again. But it is too late; I have no claim to the time and the health to do that. What I did is already enough. It may be too much, I don't know. It will depended largely on the reception of the last book. If it is not well-received I think that I will keep silent.

REAGAN: It is likely to be received differently in the United States than in France, but I think it will be very well-received here.

RICOEUR: Do you think so? I have been told that in France it will not be well-received. For two reasons: some will say that the audience has changed. The philosophical scene in France has totally changed. And also the fact that I discuss so many Anglo-Saxon authors whom they have not read. So many people will be infuriated by the fact that I know more than they know—this was always my problem.

REAGAN: Well, *La Métaphore vive* was the same way, half of the authors were Anglo-Saxon, the other half French, so you could guarantee that one-half of all of your audience didn't understand half of the book. Only it was a different half that wasn't understood.

RICOEUR: But I would have hoped that even if only half of them understood, they would have understood the other part, that is, the French would understand the Anglo-Saxon part. By the way, since I discuss at length Davidson and Parfit, I don't know how they will react to that.

REAGAN: Maybe the Germans will be the only ones who can understand the whole.

RICOEUR: Yes, Yes. The German translation will be made by Jean Greisch, who is a great Germanist. He is Luxembourgian, and he has been raised in German. So he is quite bilingual and he is even more at ease in German than French. He is completely bilingual. With the computer, he will read the text and write it down directly in German. It will read as a German text, and I think he will do that very quickly. He knows very well what I am doing; we are very close to one another.

As a young philosopher, so many decades ago, I sketched out a plan for my work. This was a very foolish thing, to planify one's work. It never works—for two reasons, at least. First because the audience has changed. I would say the philosophical scene has completely changed from the time when I started, let us say when existentialism was the leading philosophy in France and phenomenology itself was understood as existential phenomenology. When I started to work and to write, Sartre and Merleau-Ponty dominated the philosophical scene, and then came the structuralists and then the Lacanians and so on, and Derrida. I had to solve the difficult problem of how to keep my own thrust and my own project and, at the same time, always take into account the surroundings. I don't know whether my readers see my work as continuous or discontinuous—to what extent I have preserved the plan.

The second reason why we have been foolish is the fact that I learned precisely problems, works, and so on which I could not imagine existing. Look, when I was a student at the Sorbonne in the 1930s, the second half of the 1930s, nobody at the Sorbonne was able to give me a course on Bertrand Russell, who had written many years before then. He was completely unknown there. So I had to discover a whole Anglo-Saxon scene. Nevertheless, I would say that I have kept something of this early project, for example, the move from, let us say, a phenomenology of the will to a poetics of action. If I called it a "poetics" in the bold sense, it makes action creative, and in that sense the book on metaphor and the book on narrative belong to this exploration of the creative aspects of imagination and language. It is true that when I sketched that plan it was more or less less influenced by the structure of Karl Jaspers' work in the three volumes of his philosophy. So what I have actually done has taken a somewhat different path, of course. I would characterize my work as an intersection of the problem of language and the problem of action. The kind of problem you are raising here is not the problem for the author. According to my own theory, the author is not the best interpreter of his own work. Then there is a problem of the relationship between work and reader. So, it is a problem for my readers. Is there a unity in my work, is it continuous or discontinuous, and are there syntheses that I proposed before completing it? Are they weak syntheses? Weaker than the opposing syntheses? This is a problem for my readers.

REAGAN: Well, as you know, in the articles that I write, I describe it as an intellectual journey that is much like our lives. It takes really unforeseeable turns which we could never imagine at one point for one reason or another.

RICOEUR: A typical change is what took place when when I reflected on what I had said about the symbolism of evil—where everything was centered on the problem of evil as sin. Now, because of the problem of suffering, I am much more struck by excessive suffering in the world. Some people say there are many more sufferers than there are culprits. But this leads us to the problems you know about. I am more inclined think of it as some unfinished God— but this is more private. This is a problem for many Jewish theologians.

REAGAN: Certainly after the Holocaust you have to raise these questions.

RICOEUR: And one project which is very interesting connects this with Whitehead and process theology. My dean, in a lecture last week, was saying that what we do adds internal meaning to what is the cosmic individual and then makes a difference, so that in that sense, there is a history involved. And, I would add suffering. But this is a private confession. It is not by chance that we spoke a while ago about compassion, because I think it is the feeling that is most lacking. And so, I don't know whether I will have the time, the health, the strength to write on these topics. At least I will not be unemployed.

REAGAN: Very good. This is an excellent addition to the previous interviews. It prepares us for the next one a couple of years hence in Paris or somewhere. Thank you, Paul.

Chatenay-Malabry, July 8, 1991

REAGAN: In the interviews that we have done during the past eight to ten years, we have discussed your works *Time and Narrative*, *Du texte à l'action*, the international conference on your work at Cérisy-la-Salle, and, in the last interview we did in Chicago last fall, we talked at length about *Soi-même comme un autre*. In this interview, I would like to talk more about your work, but especially about your life. For example, when you were young, you envisioned a trilogy, an eidetics, a pragmatics, and a poetics of the will. Looking back, do you think your work resembles an architectonic or is it, rather, an intellectual journey? Or, choose another metaphor.

RICOEUR: Yes, yes. The trilogy that I proposed in the preface to the philosophy of the will is clearly inspired by the trilogy in the philosophy of Karl Jaspers, on which I had worked with Mikel Dufrenne, during the five years of captivity from 1940 to 1945. This work resulted, by the way, in a jointly authored book on Jaspers. My proposed trilogy corresponded closely to the three parts of the philosophy of Jaspers. In his trilogy, the first part was called "Exploration of the World," the second "Existence," and the third "Transcendence and Metaphysics." This is the format I planned for my future work.

I deviated from this plan because of the development of the philosophy of the will itself. That is to say, I began with a reflexive method borrowed from Husserl, with a certain existential influence similar to that of Merleau-Ponty. Nevertheless, the kind of analysis was essentially reflexive and Husserlian in the sense that reflection reaches not contingent or transitory states of consciousness but the principal structures of the mental [*psychique*] life. For example, perception, the project, or emotion, what Husserl called eidetic analysis.

The break with this method came from the recognition of the problem of evil as a fundamental structure of the will. In a sense, that could still appear as the development of the initial project because there is an empirical character of the forms of evil, whether it is a question of violence, of lies, or of certain destructive emotions. Thus, it could be said that this is the second part of the project. But the real change in the initial method came from fundamental experiences revolving around what could be called bad will rather than from language itself or direct reflexive language concerning the structure of the project, of habits, of emotion. These experiences have been structured around history and culture in general, or around the stories and myths based on symbolic language. It is, thus, the symbolism of evil—that is the title of the book—which marked the change to what could be called the hermeneutic method in my work.

This symbolism of evil, as I just said, remained partially in the envisioned framework as announced in the preface to the philosophy of the will. But, in fact, the continued goal is less important than the change in method. I have explained this much later, in particular in the first article in *Du Texte à l'action*, as what I call the grafting of hermeneutics onto phenomenology. For, on the one hand, I maintain that there is a continuity in hermeneutic phenomenology to the extent that hermeneutics remains fundamentally an understanding of the self. Thus, it remains reflexive. But, on the other hand, the means of understanding are no longer those of a transcendental or eidetic reflection but require understanding, interpretation, and thus a mode of intelligibility other than that of the immediate and intuitive grasping of the essence of mental phenomena.

As for the third part of the plan, its realization is the least evident. Nevertheless, I would claim that what I have already called a poetics of the will was accomplished in other modalities, and I will give three examples. One instance is *The Rule of Metaphor,* that is, the creativity in language on the semantic level; another instance is *Time and Narrative,* which is also concerned with creativity in language on the level of the construction of plots. Finally, there is an investigation of the social imagination under the form of *Ideology and Utopia.* In a sense, these three works cover a large part of the field of poetics.

However, the point where the poetics does not respond to the announced plan is obviously the recourse to transcendence. That is in Jaspers, under the secularized form of religion. But, on this point, my philosophy is strictly agnostic, as I said at the end of *Soi-même comme un autre.* The phenomenon, the experience, which would be closest to the experience of transcendence, such as the experience of a moral conscience, can be interpreted in multiple ways. The conscience, as an interior voice, could be that of my ancestors, that of my deepest being as Heidegger claims, or the word of a living God. But philosophy leaves open these possibilities. That is the point of intersection between the properly philosophical dimension and the properly religious dimension.

But I think that your second question bears on this point.

REAGAN: My second question is that you were raised in a devout Protestant family and you have remained in the faith as a believer and participant. The question is, then, what is the relation—if there is one—between your faith and your philosophy?

RICOEUR: I am very committed to the autonomy of philosophy and I think that in none of my works do I use any arguments borrowed from the domain of Jewish or Christian biblical writings. And, if one does use these writings, it is not an argument from authority. I mean that, for example, I put on the same plane Greek tragedy or the histories of Israel, neo-Platonic metaphysical speculations or the patristic interpretations of biblical writing. As a consequence, there is no privileged place for religion in general, or for the Judeo-Christian tradition, in philosophical argumentation.

But, if someone says, "Yes, but if you weren't Christian, if you did not recognize yourself as belonging to the movement of biblical literature, you would not have been interested in the problem of evil or, perhaps, in the poetic aspect in the broadest sense, or the creative aspect of human thought." Well, to this objection, I make all the concessions one wants by saying that no one knows where the ideas which organize oneself philosophically come from. We are all "visited"—if I can say so—by projects, by thoughts, and no one can entirely account for the ultimate motivation of his speculative interests. And, on this point, I am not found wanting; I am not any worse off than anyone else. No one is the master of the origin of his thoughts.

But that for which we are responsible are the arguments. So I have distinguished quite clearly, I think, in the preface of my most recent book, between

United States. When I came back from captivity in 1945, I was invited to teach in a small Protestant college which was supported by American pacifists, the Quakers. It is they who introduced me to the United States because my first teaching post there was at Haverford College, which is a Quaker school. If you will, there is a Quaker pacifist side of me which comes out now and then.

Then, too, perhaps my problems as Doyen at Nanterre are explained by that, because on the one side I was very sympathetic with certain leftist ideas which found their roots in my pacifist heritage from my teenage years, and, on the other side, I had a very strong sense of responsibility for the institution of which I was in charge. This is what I often call my Hegelian idea of the institution. So there is for me a small case of schizophrenia which has tormented me much more than the preceding case between philosophy and religion.

REAGAN: But was it internalized at the beginning of the Second World War, before you were taken prisoner?

RICOEUR: You know that the war was very short for us. But, yes, you are right to ask the question because almost the first time I doubted my own political choices was at the moment of the defeat. When I was with the army units from Brittany—very, very courageous—who were still in the east of France while the Germans were already in Paris, and saw those soldiers fleeing, abandoning their weapons and mixing in with the civilian population, and officers deserting their troops, I said to myself that that is the product of a kind of pacifism, a pacifism partially responsible for the defeat.

I am well aware that the defeat should not be explained by feelings, by emotions, because I saw after that, in 1945, as a prisoner, the defeat of Germany in the east and the same kind of terror among the civilians and the total disintegration of the army. The disintegration of an army reflects the political disintegration of a country. Then again, I do not want to be overcome by my minuscule responsibility, but I lived it, at least I interiorized the defeat as a certain moral judgment against myself. But you could say that those are my Protestant ideas of guilt; I am listening. I will listen to every interpretation.

REAGAN: But for weeks you were a soldier and ready to do whatever was necessary.

RICOEUR: I do not have a bad conscience as a soldier. It was a two-week war. I was captured in the common, habitual way: an encircled army, reduced to small units, scattered pockets being taken one after the other by overwhelming numbers, by aerial attacks, by tanks. So, you are lost in a field in the countryside with twenty others, surrounded by heavily armed enemy; you are dead or you are a prisoner. One could say that you could always choose death. So, there is no heroism in being a prisoner.

REAGAN: It may also be a painful subject for you, but at the height of your career at the Sorbonne, you chose to go to Nanterre.

RICOEUR: Oh, it is not a painful subject. No, I have become a spectator of myself there; no, I am quite at ease.

REAGAN: Was it with the hope of changing the university? At that time, you had written many articles on reforming the university.

RICOEUR: I think I can say that I foresaw, certainly not the events, but the outline of the crisis in the university which, in my view, revolved around three phenomena: First, demographics; the fact that we had gone from a university of the elite to a university of the masses. Second, the inappropriate institutional character of the university which was incapable of making these changes, given its rigid administrative structure and the system of examinations which consisted of a series of elimination tests. Third, the absence of any relation of closeness between professor and student. I remember that at the Sorbonne—which was built at the end of the last century—no room was provided for student meetings and the professors did not even have offices. We saw students and colleagues in the hallways, doorways, or in the courtyard of the Sorbonne. So, we had ever growing masses of students literally abandoned to themselves, without the possibility of speaking personally to a professor.

That is why I chose to go to this new institution, with the hope that it would have a much greater autonomy of functioning. That is where I was mistaken; it was nothing but a projection of the Sorbonne in miniature. The faults of the institution were less visible because there were fewer students, easier personal relationships, offices for the professors, things of that nature. But the whole curriculum of studies was exactly the same.

At the same time, this was a weak institution. And that is what leftists like Cohn-Bendit understood perfectly. Because it was the weakest institution, it was the first that had to be broken. The relationship between Nanterre and Cohn-Bendit was not entirely by chance. Perhaps it was completely contingent that he was a student there; I am not certain. Being there, he saw clearly that it was the weak point. He was the victim of an illusion analogous to our own blindness, thinking that all of the institutions of a country form a kind of a chain, as in the "Domino Theory" (like you had in your foreign policy . . . if Vietnam is lost, then . . .).

He thought that if the weakest institution were brought down, then, little by little, all the institutions would crumble. And, to a certain extent, he was almost right because the great crisis of the university became a national crisis with 11 million strikers in the streets, and General de Gaulle vacillated and was carried along on the wave. It was clearly by the force of his character that he succeeded in regrouping his own troops. Finally, public opinion got fed up with disorder and shifted in the other direction.

I think that the French university is the only one of all the universities in the world which was struck by this crisis. This was not the case at Berkeley, nor in Tokyo, nor at Berlin. It was only the French university which was truly brought to its knees. In a certain sense, it was a good thing, because we were able to reconstruct a much more flexible university system. Let me give you an example. The University of Paris, considered as a single university, had 200 thousand students, with a single rector, invisible in his office. Such was the case that decisions at the Sorbonne or at Nanterre had to be made there, without the responsibility or authority which belonged to the rector at the top. Some choices—completely absurd, like calling the police to the Sorbonne—were not made by someone on the scene who had the authority to decide on other options.

So, after that, a much more adaptive system of authority was reconstructed. There are now thirteen universities instead of only one. There is a president and an administrative council responsible at each one. The only two responsibilities we do not have are financial—because we live under the budget of the state—and the naming of professors because that is based on a national commission. Thirdly, we grant degrees on a national level because diplomas are not diplomas of the university but national diplomas. Thus, the system remains very centralized, although more decentralized, more distributed, than before the crisis of 1968.

REAGAN: You were just speaking of calling the police. Wasn't that at the crisis at Nanterre two years later, in the spring of 1970?

RICOEUR: More like 1969. I was the assistant to the Doyen in 1968 and since I was at his side during his decisions, I was rather "visible." In 1969 when the trouble started again, it was of a completely different nature than in 1968. In 1968, there was truly a revolutionary project—absurd, no doubt, but real. Cohn-Bendit dreamed of a profound change in society and its institutions.

In 1969, that was not at all the case. It was the vanquished of 1968 who, in the end, had the project of preventing the university from functioning. It is important to see that. Thus, I found myself face to face with leftists without a project, unless it was a project to destroy. And there, I found again my previous dilemma, torn between the willingness to understand, to negotiate, and, on the other hand, a very strong feeling of duty with respect to that institution.

Ultimately, I think that I was elected Doyen because the university council saw in me a kind of double character, simultaneously able to negotiate and having a rigorousness of decision. That worked for one year. I never had any protection in my office—it was invaded several times. Then, the troubles became dangerous—there were groups armed with iron bars who confronted each other. There were the ultra-leftist Maoïsts and, on the other side, the elements of the extreme right. I was literally crushed between these two pressures. And, since I refused to call the police, it was the central administration which imposed it on me. One day I found the police on the campus. I considered that a failure. I did prevent the police from entering the buildings, and so it was in those circumstances that I resigned.

REAGAN: René Rémond told me that what you did was to "banalize" the university, that is, make it possible for the police to come on the campus. But that it was the Minister of the Interior who sent an army of police in order to embarrass you.

RICOEUR: Yes, I think that this decision—which I did not agree with—resulted from my panic-stricken advice. "Banalize" means that security on the campus is no longer the responsibility of the university. You are familiar with Nanterre; it is rather large. We could not control it. We left the security and order on the campus to the police, and we assumed responsibility for order inside the buildings. It was this division of responsibility which was so ill-fated, because the police occupied all of the open space, putting the university in a state of seige. That was dangerous for them because the students in the buildings threw down on them typewriters, tables, chairs, and all sorts of objects. I was afraid that someone would get killed.

René Rémond was, at that time, my vice-Doyen and he succeeded me. He was successful where I failed.

REAGAN: But, he told me that he thought you were very successful, and if you had held on for a few more days. . . . He said that it was not he who succeeded in putting an end to the war between the students and the police. It was "self-limiting."

RICOEUR: That's possible.

REAGAN: After you resigned, you took a leave of absence for three years from the French university and you taught at the University of Louvain and the University of Chicago. Why these two universities, and how did these universities change your work?

RICOEUR: I distinguish between Louvain and Chicago; they resulted from different decisions. I chose Louvain, first because of proximity to Paris, and so it did not pose any problems of moving; but mostly because it is the center of phenomenological studies. I could take up again my research on Husserl and the phenomenological movement.

With respect to Chicago, my relation predates these events. In fact, I went to Chicago for the first time in 1967 or 1968—if I am not mistaken—and I received an honorary doctorate at the same time as Lévi-Strauss and Raymond Aron. At that time, I was invited to return regularly to teach. So my relation with Chicago has nothing to do with the crisis at Nanterre. I had already taught for two semesters at Chicago before the crisis at Nanterre. Afterwards, it was easier to divide my time between France and the United States.

The person who was the most instrumental in my choice of Chicago was Mircea Eliade, who held the chair of the comparative history of religions. I had known him since 1947, when he was in Paris, teaching at the Ecole pratique des Hautes Etudes. So, it was a very old friendship. My choice of the University of Chicago was also motivated by the fact that I could teach simultaneously in the Department of Philosophy, the Divinity School, and the Committee on Social Thought. It was there that I met Hannah Arendt at the home of Paul Tillich. My friendship in those days with Paul Tillich and Hannah Arendt played a major role in the decision of the University of Chicago to invite me to regularly give courses there. We were speaking a little bit ago about the schizophrenia between philosophy and theology. Well, I could live this schizophrenia institutionally in the Divinity School since I held a chair with a schizophrenic title; it was called "theological philosophy" or "philosophical theology." I don't remember which.

REAGAN: And you followed Tillich in this chair?

RICOEUR: Yes, that's right; I succeeded him in what is called the "John Nuveen Chair."

REAGAN: But was your work changed as well by meeting English and American philosophers and reading their books?

RICOEUR: Yes, yes. I date my interest in analytic philosophy back much further than that. During the 1960s at the Sorbonne, I taught courses on Russell, on Ryle, and, after that, on Austin, and speech-act theory. So my interest in English philosophy is rather old. Paradoxically, it was Husserl who led me to it because he always took seriously what was called in those days, "empiricism." I gave courses in the history of philosophy—during the time I was at Strasbourg, between 1948 and 1957—and on Hume and Berkeley.

It became even more necessary, if I may say so, from the fact of having students at Chicago whose philosophical formation was completely analytic. But it was only relatively recently that I integrated analytic philosophy as a means in my own philosophy, on the basis of this hermeneutic argument: There is no direct knowledge of the self, only that which passes through the intermediary of norms, of symbols. Thus, the objective analyses, whether of action or of personal identity, which I find in analytic philosophy, nourish for me this indirect reflection. I explain this in *The Self as Another*. The detour through analytic philosophy is one more detour in a method which rests on detours. Detour/return is the rhythm of my philosophical respiration. But I have always been very sensitive to the force of argumentation in analytic philosophy, which seems to me to accord completely with the great conceptual concerns that Husserl had, and which phenomenologists after him did not always share.

REAGAN: After twenty years of teaching at the University of Chicago and giving lectures all over the United States and all over the world, your work has been recently rediscovered in France these past few years. For example, three years ago there was the international conference at Cérisy-la-Salle on your work. Most recently, you have received the prize in philosophy from the French Institute. It is like having two careers in France.

RICOEUR: I am not the judge; I am not the historian of myself. I have never suffered because of a lack of recognition, perhaps for a reason having to do with my style of writing. I can be criticized because I have never paid attention to my audience. I mean that my way of writing my philosophical books responds to an interior need, comes from questions that are imposed on me which I cannot escape. I remember that it was the first piece of advice I received from my very first professor of philosophy: when there is an obstacle, do not go around it, go right at it. So, I have a combative style, not of hostility—on the contrary, a kind of sympathy—for my adversary, which means that I always chose my opponents for reasons other than they are popular, "new philosophers," or in the news. In the end, I explain myself through my best adversaries and it is rather a debate with myself, without considering how my books will be received by the public.

I think that I have a very good reputation as a teacher. And, down deep, I am more satisfied with my career because I helped in the philosophical education of several generations of students. My relation with a larger public constitutes a different history with a rather later but more complete recognition. Perhaps that's the benefit of age.

REAGAN: Finally, one last question. Last week when Antenne 2 television was taping those long interviews with you, we all had a good laugh when you told how General de Gaulle said during an interview, "You have neglected to ask me the best question which is this. . . ." Then he would ask himself a question and proceed to answer it. So, I want to give you the chance to do like de Gaulle and ask a question of yourself.

RICOEUR: Perhaps we could talk about my future projects. It is a very difficult situation when one has finished a book. There is a period which resembles the depression which comes after giving birth. The problem is more serious at my age. I must say that I have three areas of interest which are not at all coordinated and I do not know if they will result in a work as structured as *Time and Narrative* or *The Self as Another.*

I would like to continue my research on the idea of justice, which has an important place in ethics and which was at the center of my last work. It so happens that I have been involved, here in France, in an institution, Ecole Nationale [National School of Jurisprudence] on the problem of justice, and also with the Commissariate au Plan [Ministry of Planning] on the problem of inequalities, and, in particular, the paradox of just inequalities—that is, are there just inequalities? So, I want to pursue my previous discussions with Rawls and Habermas on this level.

The discussion is actually at an impasse between an abstract and procedural universalism in the style of John Rawls, or in a different but parallel way in Habermas, and a communitarianism based on concrete historical experience. I am captivated by this discussion, this debate. I would like to research further the implications of the idea of justice under its formal, institutional, historic, and concrete aspects. That is one field of research with an annex of exploring the emotions as structuring the social or public space, in the manner of Hirschman and others. And, with always the same problem, that of finding a living content to the abstract rules of judicial procedure, or a transcendental pragmatic in the style of Habermas. All of that is a whole.

Second, I have turned again to my studies of historiography, with two interests. One is how rationality functions in the reconstruction of history; the other is the status of the past which was but which is no longer and so escapes the criteria of verification, but which, nevertheless, has a kind of weight of reality. So, I have been working on a hundred-page monograph which will be published by the Institut International de Philosophie [International Institute of Philosophy].

The third domain is research on the transition between biblical exegesis and philosophical reflection on the level which I previously called my "schizophrenia." I claim that there is an intelligibility at work in these texts of exegesis and the function of exegesis is to articulate this intelligibility. I have always maintained the idea that language, discourse, has a multitude of functions. In this sense, I am completely on the side of Wittgenstein in his *Philosophical Investigations,* where language games have an unlimited world and philosophy has, among others, the responsibility to preserve the autonomy, the rights, of these language games. There is a place for religious language alongside poetic language alongside scientific language.

It is in the perspective of this pluralism of the forms of discourse that one can explore the intersections, the interferences among these spheres. There are certainly relations between ethics and religion, for example, on the level of *agape*, or love. I did a small work on love and justice which anticipates this. But there is also between historical intelligibility—given the enormous place of historical writing—some poetic intersections with poetic discourse, with biblical lyricism, as in the Book of Job. In this respect, I am very interested in a comparison between the Psalms and Greek tragedy, on the level of the complaint or lamentation. We have not talked about the problem which haunts me more and more—and which is taking the place of the problem of evil or of guilt: the evil of suffering, and the problem of the suffering man. In my works, I always speak of man acting and suffering.

Finally, events in my personal life and the spectacle of the world have made me sensitive to the fact that there is widespread unmerited suffering in the world. There is a language to be found. It is the problem of Auschwitz, the problem of memory and forgiveness. I am interested in exploring the areas of intersection between the religious, the poetic, the ethical, and the historical. I think that I have paid sufficiently for their distinction that I have the right to say something about their conjunction. At my age, that is enough projects.

(*Unlike the previous interviews, which were conducted in English, this interview was done in French. The French version has been previously published in* Bulletin de la Société Américaine de Philosophie de Langue Française, *3, no. 3 [Winter 1991]: 155–72.*)

BIBLIOGRAPHY

ALL RICOEUR SCHOLARS are indebted to the extraordinary work of Franz D. Vansina in compiling a complete bibliography of Paul Ricoeur's writings. Included in Father Vansina's bibliography are all of Ricoeur's major works, articles, published letters, sermons, and minor works published in sectarian or local reviews and journals. He has also included all of the translations of Ricoeur's books and articles. And he has compiled a virtually complete bibliography of books and articles about Ricoeur. His work is entitled *Paul Ricoeur: A Primary and Secondary Systematic Bibliography (1935–1984)* (Leuven: Editions Peeters, 1985). Vansina's bibliography has been updated and reprinted in *The Philosophy of Paul Ricoeur* (Library of Living Philosophers, vol. 22), ed. Louis E. Hahn (Chicago: Open Court, 1995). Since this excellent and complete bibliography is available, I do not attempt to duplicate it here.

This bibliography is intended for an English-speaking audience. Thus, I will give the bibliographic information for the English translation first, and then the original French source. For articles, I will list only the most important ones, and only the English version. I will follow the same rule with secondary sources.

Major Works by Ricoeur

Freedom and Nature: The Voluntary and the Involuntary. Translated by E. V. Kohak. Evanston: Northwestern University Press, 1966. *Le Volontaire et l'involontaire.* Paris: Aubier, 1950.

Fallible Man. Translated by Charles Kelbley. Chicago: Henry Regnery, 1965. *Finitude et Culpabilité I: L'homme faillible.* Paris: Aubier, 1960.

The Symbolism of Evil. Translated by Emerson Buchanan. New York: Harper and Row, 1967; reprinted, Boston: Beacon Press, 1969. *Finitude et Culpabilité II: La Symbolique du mal.* Paris: Aubier, 1960.

Freud and Philosophy: An Essay on Interpretation. Translated by Dennis Savage. New Haven: Yale University Press, 1970. *De l'interprétation. Essai sur Freud.* Paris: Le Seuil, 1965.

The Rule of Metaphor. Multi-Disciplinary Studies of the Creation of Meaning in Language. Translated by R. Czerny with K. McLaughlin and J. Costello. Toronto: University of Toronto Press, 1978. *La métaphore vive.* Paris: Le Seuil, 1975.

Time and Narrative. Vol. 1. Translated by K. McLaughlin and D. Pellauer. Chicago: University of Chicago Press, 1984. *Temps et récit. Tome 1.* Paris: Le Seuil, 1983.

Time and Narrative. Vol. 2. Translated by K. McLaughlin and D. Pellauer. Chicago: University of Chicago Press, 1985. *Temps et récit. Tome 2. La configuration dans le récit de fiction.* Paris: Le Seuil, 1984.

Time and Narrative. Vol. 3. Translated by K. Blamey and D. Pellauer. Chicago: University of Chicago Press, 1988. *Temps et récit. Tome 3. Le temps raconté.* Paris: Le Seuil, 1985.

Oneself as Another. Translated by K. Blamey. Chicago: University of Chicago Press, 1992. *Soi-même comme un autre.* Paris: Le Seuil, 1990.

Collections of His Articles Edited by Ricoeur

History and Truth. Translated by C. Kelbley and others. Evanston: Northwestern University Press, 1965. *Histoire et vérité.* Paris: Le Seuil, 1955.

The Conflict of Interpretations. Essays in Hermeneutics. Edited by D. Ihde. Evanston: Northwestern University Press, 1974. *Le conflit des interprétations. Essais d'herméneutique.* Paris: Le Seuil, 1969.

From Text to Action. Essays in Hermeneutics, II. Translated by K. Blamey and J. Thompson. Evanston: Northwestern University Press, 1991. *Du texte à l'action. Essais d'herméneutique, II.* Paris: Le Seuil, 1986.

Collections of Ricoeur's Articles and Writings Edited by Others

Husserl: An Analysis of His Phenomenology. Translated and edited by E. G. Ballard and L. E. Embree. Evanston: Northwestern University Press, 1967.

Tragic Wisdom and Beyond, including *Conversations between Paul Ricoeur and Gabriel Marcel.* Translated by P. McCormick and S. Jolin. Evanston: Northwestern University Press, 1973.

Political and Social Essays. Edited by D. Stewart and J. Bien. Athens: Ohio University Press, 1974.

The Philosophy of Paul Ricoeur. An Anthology of His Work. Edited by C. Reagan and D. Stewart. Boston: Beacon Press, 1978.

Essays on Biblical Interpretation. Edited by L. Mudge. Philadelphia: Fortress Press, 1980.

Hermeneutics and the Human Sciences. Edited and translated by J. B. Thompson. Cambridge: Cambridge University Press, 1980.

Lectures on Ideology and Utopia. Edited by G. H. Taylor (edited transcripts of a course given by Paul Ricoeur at the University of Chicago). New York: Columbia University Press, 1986.

A Ricoeur Reader: Reflection and Imagination. Edited by M. Valdés. Toronto: University of Toronto Press, 1991.

Other Books by Ricoeur

Interpretation Theory: Discourse and the Surplus of Meaning. Fort Worth: Texas Christian University Press, 1976.

Main Trends in Philosophy. Edited by Paul Ricoeur. New York and London: Holmes and Meier, 1979.

The Contribution of French Historiography to the Theory of History (The Zaharoff Lecture for 1978–79). Oxford: Clarendon Press, 1980.

Major Articles by Ricoeur

Vansina's bibliography lists 519 published articles, prefaces, letters, etc. in French, many
of which were originally written in English and then translated into French. Most of
Ricoeur's most important articles are in one of the collections edited by himself or
by others. The following bibliography is highly selective.

"The Symbol . . . Food for Thought." *Philosophy Today* 4, no. 3/4, Fall (1960):
196–207.

"The Hermeneutics of Symbols and Philosophical Reflection." *International Philosophical Quarterly* 2, no. 2 (1962): 191–218.

"The Historical Presence of Non-violence." *Cross Currents* 14, no. 1, Winter (1964):
15–23.

"The Atheism of Freudian Psychoanalysis." *Concilium* 2, no. 16 (1966): 59–72.

"Kant and Husserl." *Philosophy Today* 10, no. 3/4, Fall (1966): 147–68.

"Philosophy of Will and Action." In *Phenomenology of Will and Action*. Edited by W.
Straus and R. M. Griffith. Pittsburgh: Duquesne University Press, 1967: 7–60.

"Husserl and Wittgenstein on Language." In *Phenomenology and Existentialism*. Edited
by E. N. Lee and M. Mandelbaum. Baltimore: John Hopkins University Press,
1967:207–17.

"The Unity of the Voluntary and the Involuntary as a Limiting Idea." In *Readings in
Existential Phenomenology*. Edited by N. Lawrence and D. O'Connor. Englewood
Cliffs: Prentice-Hall, 1967: 93–112.

"The Antinomy of Human Reality and the Problem of Philosophical Anthropology." In
Readings in Existential Phenomenology. Edited by N. Lawrence and D. O'Connor.
Englewood Cliffs: Prentice-Hall, 1967: 390–402.

"New Developments in Phenomenology in France: The Phenomenology of Language."
Social Research 34, no. 1, Spring (1967): 1–30.

"Structure-Word-Event." *Philosophy Today* 12, no. 2/4, Summer (1968): 114–29.

"The Father Image. From Phantasy to Symbol." *Criterion* 8, no. 1, Fall/Winter (1968):
1–7.

"The Problem of the Double-Sense as Hermeneutic Problem and as Semantic Problem." In *Myths and Symbols. Studies in Honor of Mircea Eliade*. Edited by M. M. Kita-
gawa and C. H. Long. Chicago-London: University of Chicago Press, 1969: 63–
79.

"Religion, Atheism and Faith" (Bampton Lectures in America, Columbia University,
1966). In *The Religious Significance of Atheism*. Edited by A. MacIntyre and P. Ricoeur. New York-London: Columbia University Press, 1969: 58–98.

"The Problem of the Will and Philosophical Discourse." In *Patterns of the Life-World*.
Essays in Honor of John Wild. Edited by J. M. Edie, F. H. Parker, and C. O. Schrag.
Evanston: Northwestern University Press, 1970: 273–89.

"What Is a Text? Explanation and Interpretation." In David M. Rasmussen, *Mythic-
Symbolic Language and Philosophical Anthropology. A Constructive Interpretation of the
Thought of Paul Ricoeur*. The Hague: Martinus Nijhoff, 1973: 135–50.

"The Model of the Text: Meaningful Action Considered as a Text." *Social Research* 38, no. 3, Fall (1971):529–62. Reprinted in *Social Research* 51, nos. 1 and 2, Spring/Summer (1984): 185–218. Also reprinted in *New Literary History* 5, no. 1 (1973): 91–117.

"From Existentialism to the Philosophy of Language" (text of an address before the Divinity School, University of Chicago, 1971). *Criterion* 10, Spring (1971): 14–18. Expanded and reprinted as "A Philosophical Journey, From Existentialism to the Philosophy of Language," in *Philosophy Today* 17, no. 2/4, Summer (1973): 88–96.

"Creativity in Language. Word. Polysemy. Metaphor"(Address delivered at Duquesne University, 1972). *Philosophy Today* 17, no. 2/4, Summer (1973): 97–111.

"The Task of Hermeneutics" (Lecture given at Princeton Theological Seminary, 1973). *Philosophy Today* 17, no. 2/4, Summer (1973):112–28.

"The Hermeneutical Function of Distantiation" (Lecture given at Princeton Theological Seminary, 1973). *Philosophy Today* 17, no. 2/4, Summer (1973): 129–41.

"Psychiatry and Moral Values." In *American Handbook of Psychiatry*. I. Edited by S. Aricti et al. Second Edition. New York: Basic Books, 1974: 976–90.

"Phenomenology of Freedom." In *Phenomenology and Philosophical Understanding*. Edited by E. Pivcevic. London-New York: Cambridge University Press, 1975: 173–94.

"Phenomenology and Hermeneutics." *Noûs* 9, no. 1 (1975): 85–102.

"Biblical Hermeneutics." *Semeia*, no. 4 (1975): 27–148.

"What is Dialectical?" In *Freedom and Morality*. The Lindley Lectures delivered at the University of Kansas. Edited by J. Bricke. Lawrence: University Press of Kansas, 1976:173–89.

"Ideology and Utopia as Cultural Imagination." *Philosophic Exchange* 2, no. 2, Summer (1976): 17–28. Reprinted in *Being Human in a Technological Age*. Edited by D. Dorchert and D. Stewart. Athens: Ohio University Press, 1979: 107–25.

"History and Hermeneutics" (Paper presented at an APA Symposion on Hermeneutics, 1976). *Journal of Philosophy* 73, no. 19 (1976): 683–95.

"Phenomenology and the Social Sciences." *The Annals of Phenomenological Sociology* 2 (1977): 145–59.

"The Question of Proof in Freud's Psychoanalytic Writings." *Journal of the American Psychoanalytic Association* 25, no. 4 (1977): 835–71.

"Writing as a Problem for Literary Criticism and Philosophical Hermeneutics." *Philosophic Exchange* 2, no. 3, Summer (1977): 3–15.

"Can There Be a Scientific Concept of Ideology?" In *Phenomenology and the Social Sciences: A Dialogue*. Edited by J. Bien. The Hague: M. Nijhoff, 1978: 44–59.

"Image and Language in Psychoanalysis." In *Psychoanalysis and Language*. Edited by J. H. Smith. New Haven-London: Yale University Press, 1978: 293–324.

"The Narrative Function." *Semeia*, no. 13 (1978): 177–202.

"The Metaphorical Process as Cognition, Imagination, and Feeling." *Critical Inquiry* (On Metaphor) 5, no.1, Fall (1978): 143–59.

"Naming God." *Union Seminary Quarterly Review* 34, no. 4, Summer (1979): 215–28.

"The Hermeneutics of Testimony." *Anglican Theological Review* 61, no. 4 (1979): 435–61.

"The Function of Fiction in Shaping Reality." *Man and World* 12, no. 2 (1979): 123–41.

"Narrative Time." *Critical Inquiry* (On Narrative) 7, no. 1, Autumn (1980):169–90.

"On Interpretation." In *Philosophy in France Today.* Edited by A. Montefiore. Cambridge-New York: Cambridge University Press, 1983: 175–97.

"Narrative and Hermeneutics." In *Essays on Aesthetics. Perspectives on the Work of Monroe Beardsley.* Edited by J. Fisher. Philadelphia: Temple University Press, 1983: 149–60.

"Action, Story, and History: On Re-reading *The Human Condition.*" *Salmagundi,* no. 60, Spring-Summer (1983):60–72.

"The Power of Speech: Science and Poetry." *Philosophy Today* 29, no. 1/4, Spring (1985): 59–70.

"History as Narrative and Practice. Peter Kemp Talks to Paul Ricoeur in Copenhagen." *Philosophy Today* 29, no. 3/4 Fall (1985): 213–22.

"Narrated Time" (first draft of the conclusions on time in the forthcoming volume 3 of *Time and Narrative. Philosophy Today* 29, no. 4/4, Winter (1985): 259–72.

"Life: A Story in Search of a Narrator." In *Facts and Values. Philosophical Reflections from Western and Non-Western Perspectives.* Edited by M. C. Doeser and J. N. Kraaj. Dordrecht: Nijhoff, 1986:121–32.

"The Self in Psychoanalysis and in Phenomenological Philosophy." *Psychoanalytic Inquiry* 6, no. 3 (1986): 437–58.

"The Teleological and Deontological Structures of Action: Aristotle and/or Kant?" In *Contemporary French Philosophy.* Edited by A. Phillips Griffiths. Cambridge-New York: Cambridge University Press, 1987: 99–111.

The Greatness and Fragility of Political Language. The Forty-Second John Findley Green Foundation Lecture (delivered at Westminster College, Fulton, Missouri, 1987). 1987.

"Greimas's Narrative Grammar." *New Literary History* 20, no. 3 (1989): 581–608.

"Interpretative Narrative." In *The Book and the Text. The Bible and Literary Theory.* Edited by R. Schwartz. Cambridge, Mass.: Blackwell, 1990: 236–57.

"Narrative Identity." *Philosophy Today* 35, no. 1/4, Spring (1991): 73–81.

"Ricoeur on Narrative." In *On Paul Ricoeur. Narrative and Interpretation.* Edited by D. Wood. London-New York: Routledge, 1991: 160–87.

"Self as Ipse." In *Freedom and Interpretation. The Oxford Amnesty Lectures, 1992.* Edited by B. Johnson. New York: Basic Books, 1993.

Intellectual Autobiographies

"A Philosophical Journey. From Existentialism to the Philosophy of Language." *Philosophy Today* 17, no. 2/4, Summer (1973): 88–96.

"Phenomenology and Hermeneutics." *Noûs* 9, no. 1 (1975): 85–102.

"On Interpretation." In *Philosophy in France Today.* Edited by A. Montefiore. Cambridge-New York: Cambridge University Press, 1983: 175–97.

"Intellectual Autobiography." Translated by K. Blamey. In *The Philosophy of Paul Ricoeur* (Library of Living Philosophers, vol. 22). Edited by Louis Hahn. Chicago: Open Court, 1995: 3–53.

Principal Secondary Sources

Albano, P. J. *Freedom, Truth and Hope. The Relationship of Philosophy and Religion in the Thought of Paul Ricoeur.* Lanham, Md.: University Press of America, 1987.

Anderson, Pamela S. *Ricoeur and Kant. Philosophy of the Will.* Atlanta: Scholars Press, 1993.

Bourgeois, P. L. *Extension of Ricoeur's Hermeneutic.* The Hague: M. Nijhoff, 1975.

Bourgeois, P. L. and Schalow, F., *Traces of Understanding: A Profile of Heidegger's and Ricoeur's Hermeneutics.* Würzburg-Amsterdam-Atlanta: Königshausen-Neumann-Rodopi, 1990.

Clark, S. H. *Paul Ricoeur.* London-New York: Routledge, 1990.

Dicenso, J. *Hermeneutics and the Disclosure of Truth. A Study in the Work of Heidegger, Gadamer and Ricoeur.* Charlottesville: University Press of Virginia, 1990.

Doran, R. M. *Subject and Psyche. Ricoeur, Jung and the Search for Foundations.* Washington, D.C.: University Press of America, 1979.

Dornisch, Loretta. *Faith and Philosophy in the Writings of Paul Ricoeur.* Lampeter-Dyfed: Edwin Meller Press, 1990.

Gerhart, Mary. *The Question of Belief in Literary Criticism. An Introduction to the Hermeneutical Theory of Paul Ricoeur.* Stuttgart: Akademischer Verlag Hans-Dieter Heinz, 1979.

Ihde, Don. *Hermeneutic Phenomenology. The Philosophy of Paul Ricoeur.* Evanston: Northwestern University Press, 1971.

Jervolino, Domenico. *The Cogito and Hermeneutics: The Question of the Subject in Ricoeur.* Translated by Gordon Poole. Dordrecht-Boston-London: Kluwer Academic Publishers, 1990.

Kemp, Peter and Rasmussen, David, ed., *The Narrative Path. The Later Works of Paul Ricoeur.* Cambridge, Mass.: MIT Press, 1989.

Klemm, D. E. *The Hermeneutical Theory of Paul Ricoeur. A Constructive Analysis.* Lewisburg: Bucknell University Press-Associated University Press, 1983.

Klemm, D. E. and Schweiker, William, eds. *Meanings in Texts and Actions. Questioning Paul Ricoeur.* Charlottsville: University Press of Virginia, 1993.

Lowe, Walter J. *Mystery of the Unconscious. A Study in the Thought of Paul Ricoeur.* Metuchen: The Scarecrow Press-The American Theological Library Association, 1977.

Ormiston, G. L. and Schrift, A. D. *The Hermeneutic Tradition. From Ast to Ricoeur.* Albany: State University of New York Press, 1990.

Rasmussen, David. *Mythic-Symbolic Language and Philosophical Anthropology. A Constructive Interpretation of the Thought of Paul Ricoeur.* The Hague: M. Nijhoff, 1971.

Reagan, Charles E., ed. *Studies in the Philosophy of Paul Ricoeur.* Athens: Ohio University Press, 1979.

Streib, H. *Hermeneutics of Metaphor, Symbol, and Narrative in Faith Development Theory.* Bern-Frankfurt am Main-New York: Verlag Peter Lang, 1991.

Thompson, John B. *Critical Hermeneutics. A Study in the Thought of Paul Ricoeur and Jürgen Habermas.* Cambridge: Cambridge University Press, 1981.

Van Den Hengel, J. H. *The Home of Meaning. The Hermeneutics of the Subject of Paul Ri-coeur.* Doctoral thesis presented at the Katholieke Universiteit of Nijmegen. Washington, D.C.: University Press of America, 1982.

Vanhoozer, K. J. *Biblical Narrative in the Philosophy of Paul Ricoeur. A Study in Hermeneutics and Theology.* Cambridge-New York-Port Chester-Melbourne-Sydney: Cambridge University Press, 1990.

Van Leeuwen, T. M. *The Surplus of Meaning. Ontology and Eschatology in the Philosophy of Paul Ricoeur.* Amsterdam: Rodopi, 1981.

Valdès, Mario, ed., *A Ricoeur Reader. Reflection and Imagination.* Toronto-Buffalo: Toronto University Press, 1991.

Wood, D. *On Paul Ricoeur. Narrative and Interpretation.* London-New York: Routledge, 1991.

Selected Articles

Note: Franz Vansina's most recent bibliography of Ricoeur lists 289 articles and book reviews in English. Thus, this list of articles is highly selective. Articles are listed in chronological order.

Ihde, Don. "From Phenomenology to Hermeneutic [on P. Ricoeur's hermeneutics]." *Journal of Existentialism* 8, No. 30, Winter (1967–68): 111–132.

Reagan, Charles E. "Ricoeur's 'Diagnostic' Relation." *International Philosophical Quarterly* 8, No. 4, December (1968): 586–592.

Stewart, David. "Paul Ricoeur and the Phenomenological Movement." *Philosophy Today* 12, No. 4/4, Winter (1968): 227–235.

Stewart, David. "Paul Ricoeur's Phenomenology of Evil." *International Philosophical Quarterly* 9, No. 4, December (1969): 572–589.

Bourgeois, Patrick. "Hermeneutics of Symbols and Philosophical Reflection: Paul Ricoeur." *Philosophy Today* 15, No. 4/4, Winter (1971): 231–241.

Bourgeois, Patrick. "Paul Ricoeur's Hermeneutical Phenomenology." *Philosophy Today* 16, No. 1/4, Spring (1972): 20–27.

Stewart, David. "The Christian and Politics: Reflections on Power in the Thought of Paul Ricoeur." *Journal of Religion* 52, No. 1, January (1972): 56–83.

Doran, R. M. "Paul Ricoeur: Toward the Restoration of Meaning." *Anglican Theological Review* 55, No. 4, October (1973): 443–458.

Stewart, David. "Language and/et langage." *Philosophy Today* 18, No. 2/4, Summer (1974): 87–105.

Scott, Charles E. "Ricoeur's Freud." *Anglican Theological Review* 57, No. 4, October (1975): 467–479.

Edie, James. "Identity and Metaphor: A Phenomenological Theory of Polysemy." *Journal of the British Society for Phenomenology* 6, No. 1, January (1975): 32–41.

Gerhart, Mary. "Paul Ricoeur's Hrmeneutical Theory as Resource for Theological Reflection." *The Thomist* 39, No. 3, July, (1975): 496–527.

Gerhart, Mary. "Paul Ricoeur's Notion of 'Diagnostics': Its Function in Literary Interpretation." *Journal of Religion* 56, No 2, April (1976): 137–156.

Pellauer, David. "A 'Response on Paul Ricoeur's Philosophy of Metaphor'." *Philosophy Today* 21, Supplement to No. 4/4, winter (1977): 437–445.

Klein, Ted. "Ricoeur and Husserl." *Iliff Review* (Special Issue. Paul Ricoeur's Philosophy) 35, No. 3, Fall (1978): 37–47.

Gehart, Mary. "Imagination and History in Ricoeur's Interpretation Theory." *Philosophy Today* 23, No. 1/4, Spring (1979): 51–68.

Lacocque, André. "Job and the Symbolism of Evil [followed by a response by Paul Ricoeur]." *Biblical Research* 24–25, (1979–1980): 7–19, 70–71.

Ihde, Don. "Interpreting Hermeneutics: Origins, Developments and Prospects." *Man and World* 13, No. 3–4 (1980): 325–343.

Kurzweil E. "IV. Paul Ricoeur. Hermeneutics and Structuralism," In *The Age of Structuralism. Lévi-Strauss to Foucault.* New York: Columbia University Press, 1980: 78–112.

Dornisch, L. "The Book of Job and Ricoeur's Hermeneutics [introduction to special issue]." *Semeia* (The Book of Job and Ricoeur's Hermeneutics), No. 19 (1981): 3–21.

Lacocque, André. "Apocalyptic Symbolism: A Ricoeurian Hermeneutical Approach." *Biblical Research* 26 (1981): 6–15.

Lowe, Walter. "The Coherence of Paul Ricoeur." *Journal of Religion* 61, No. 4 (1981): 384–402.

Pellauer, David. "Paul Ricoeur on the Specificity of Religious Language." *Journal of Religion* 61, No. 3 (1981): 264–284.

Dauenhauer, B. P. "Ricoeur's Metaphor Theory and Some of Its Consequences." *Southern Journal of Philosophy* 12, Spring (1983): 1–12.

Schwartz, S. "Hermeneutics and the Productive Imagination: Paul Ricoeur in the 1970s." *Journal of Religion* 63, No. 3, July (1983): 290–300.

Reagan, Charles E. "Hermeneutics and the Semantics of Action." *Pre/Text* 4, No. 3–4, Fall-Winter (1983): 239–255.

Barral, M. R. "Paul Ricoeur: The Resurrection as Hope and Freedom." *Philosophy Today* 29, No. 1/4, Spring (1985): 72–82.

Madison, G. B. "Text and Action: The Hermeneutics of Existence." *Revue de l'Université d'Ottawa. University of Ottawa Quarterly* 55, No. 4, October-December (1985): 135–145.

Valdés, Mario J. "Paul Ricoeur's Phenomenological Hermeneutics as a Basis for Literary Criticism." *Revue de l'Université d'Ottawa. University of Ottawa Quarterly* 55, No. 4, October-December (1985): 115–126.

Kearney, Richard. "Paul Ricoeur." In *Modern Movements in European Philosophy.* Manchester: Manchester University Press, 1986: 91–112.

Bourgeois, P. And Schalow, F. "Hermeneutics of Existence: Conflict and Resolution." *Philosophy Today* 31, No. 1/4, Spring (1987): 45–53.

Pellauer, David. "Some Preliminary Reflections. *Time and Narrative* and Theological Reflection." *Philosophy Today* 31, No. 3/4, Fall (1987): 262–286.

Joy, M. "Derrida and Ricoeur. A Case of Mistaken Identity (and Difference)." *Journal of Religion* 68, No. 4 (1988): 508–526.

Michell, L. "History and Imagination in the Philosophy of Paul Ricoeur." *Southern Journal of Philosophy* 8, No. 1 (1989): 41–49.

Kellner, H. "As real as it gets . . . Ricoeur and Narrativity." *Philosophy Today* 34, No. 3/4, Fall (1990): 229–242.

Lawlor, L. "The Dialectical Unity of Hermeneutics: on Ricoeur and Gadamer." In *Gadamer and Hermeneutics*. Edited with an introduction by H. J. Silverman. New York-London: Routledge, 1991: 82–90.

Reagan, Charles E. "The Self as Another." *Philosophy Today* 37, No. 1, Spring (1993): 3–22.

Abel, Olivier. "Ricoeur's ethics of Method." *Philosophy Today* 37, No. 1, Spring (1993): 23–30.

Bourgeois, Patrick. "The Instant and the Living Present: Ricoeur and Derrida Reading Husserl." *Philosophy Today* 37, No. 1, Spring (1993): 31–37.

INDEX

Abel, Olivier, 68, 69

abortion, 93

action: and agent, 79–82; analytical philosophy of, 45, 50, 54, 75, 80–81; causes of versus reasons for, 81; chains of actions, 80; language and, 75; moral imputation of an action to an agent, 82; narrative and, 19, 76, 119; poetics of, 122; the power to act, 82, 90; in Ricoeur's work, 19, 41, 45; suffering and, 64, 76, 85, 88, 113, 135; three ways of speaking about, 118; tragedy of, 92, 94; voluntary action, 18

adverbs of time and place, 78

agents, 79–82

Algeria, 24–25, 127

Alter, Robert, 121

analytical philosophy: of action, 45, 50, 54, 75, 80–81; in France, 110; hermeneutics and, 96; and redescribing the world, 107; Ricoeur's interest in, 132

Anscombe, G. E. M., 80, 81

Antigone (Sophocles), 92

Arendt, Hannah, 132

argumentation, 95

Aristotle: and attestation, 97; on friendship, 87; on the golden mean, 89; on proportional justice, 92, 119; on the question "why?" 81; teleological ethics of, 50, 86; on time, 47

attestation, 67, 76–77, 81, 97, 98

"Attestation: Between Phenomenology and Ontology" (Ricoeur), 67

Augustine, Saint, 47, 111

Austin, John, 79, 132

authority, 102

autonomy, 89, 90, 91, 94

Baboulène, Jean, 21

bad conscience, 98

Barth, Karl, 29, 41

Being and Nothingness (Sartre), 17–18

Bennington, Geoffrey, 69

Berkeley, George, 132

Betti, Emilio, 115

Bible, 121

biblical faith, 78

biblical hermeneutics, 121

Birault, Henri, 52

Black, Max, 106

Blum, Léon, 127

bracketing, 103

Bultmann, Rudolf, 29, 41

Camus, Albert, 15

categorical imperative, 90, 93, 114

causality, efficient, 82

Cavaillès, Jean, 19

Centre National de Recherche Scientifique (CNRS), 32

Chambon-sur-Lignon, Le, 14–15

character, 84

Christian socialism, 6, 19, 126

classics, 102

cogito, 74–75, 76, 96

Cohn-Bendit, Daniel, 33, 69, 129, 130

configuration, 85

Conflict of Interpretations, The. Essays in Hermeneutics (*Le Conflit des interprétations. Essais d'herméneutique;* Ricoeur), 39, 117

conscience, 97, 98–99, 125

"conscient et l'inconscient, Le" (Ricoeur), 26

consent, 10, 18–19

consolation, 29, 41

constatives, 79

contextualism, 94, 95

Contribution of French Historiography to the Theory of History, The (Ricoeur), 44

conviction, 95

corps propre (lived body), 18, 82

Dalbiez, Roland, 5, 26

Davidson, Donald, 82, 96, 97, 121

"Décade de Paul Ricoeur" (colloquium), 66–68, 115–16, 117–18

deconstructionism, 55–56, 110

definite descriptions, 78, 80

De l'interprétation. Essai sur Freud (*Freud and Philosophy;* Ricoeur), 26, 27–30, 68

democracy, 93

demonstratives, 78, 80

deontology, 50, 86, 89, 91, 95

Derrida, Jacques, 43, 44, 56, 59, 62, 69, 122

Descartes, René, 74, 75, 76, 96, 99

description, 76, 83, 85, 106–7, 118, 119

descriptions, definite, 78, 80

dialectics, 99

Dilthey, Wilhelm, 46, 101–2, 104

distributive justice, 89, 90, 98

Domenach, Jean-Marie, 21

Dufrenne, Mikel, 9, 15, 123

Du texte à l'action. Essais d'herméneutique, II (From Text to Action. Essays in Hermeneutics, 2; Ricoeur), 49, 65, 73, 117

efficient causality, 82

eidetic method, 17, 18, 124

Eliade, Christinel, 41, 64

Eliade, Mircea, 29, 41, 64, 121, 132

equality, 87, 88, 134

Esprit (journal), 19, 21, 22, 25, 40, 59

ethics, 86–96; of argumentation, 95; the good life as the aim of, 86; as independent of religion, 120; the moral distinguished from the ethical, 86; narration and, 85; politics and, 118–19; Ricoeur approaching from point of view of the victim, 113; Ricoeur's dialectic between Aristotle and Kant, 50. *See also* morals

event, 85

evil, 23–24, 89, 123, 124

existentialism, 110, 122

"Explanation and Understanding: On Some Remarkable Connections Among the Theory of Text, Theory of Action, and Theory of History" (Ricoeur), 45–46, 49

"Faire l'Université" ("To Make the University"; Ricoeur), 31

faith, biblical, 78

Fallible Man (Ricoeur), 23, 25, 29, 84

feelings, 120

Finitude and Culpability (Finitude et Culpabilité; Ricoeur), 23, 28; *Fallible Man,* 23, 25, 29, 84; *The Symbolism of Evil,* 23–24, 25, 26, 40

flesh, the, 97

foundationalism, 75, 96, 99

Fraisse, Paul, 21

Frankfurt school, 102, 110

Freedom and Nature: The Voluntary and the Involuntary (Le Volontaire et l'involontaire; Ricoeur), 17–19; chapter on the unconscious, 26; on character, 84; as modeled on Jaspers, 9; outlines and

first drafts in Ricoeur's camp journals, 10, 16, 66; as a theory of action, 117

Freud, Sigmund, 26, 27, 29, 40, 75, 105

Freud and Philosophy (De l'interprétation. Essai sur Freud; Ricoeur), 26, 27–30, 68

friendship, 87–88, 98

From Text to Action. Essays in Hermeneutics, 2 (Du texte à l'action. Essais d'herméneutique, II; Ricoeur), 49, 65, 73, 117

Gabriel Marcel et Karl Jaspers: Philosophie du mystère et philosophie du paradox (Ricoeur), 16

Gadamer, Hans, 101, 102–3, 108

Gewirth, Alan, 113

Gifford Lectures, 48–49, 65, 74, 112–14, 118

golden mean, 89

Golden Rule, 90

good conscience, 98–99

good life, the, 50, 86–87, 89, 92

Goodman, Nelson, 107

good will, 89

Grappin, Pierre, 33

Greisch, Jean, 66, 67, 116, 117, 120, 122

Guichard, Olivier, 36, 38

guilt, 27, 29, 41

Habermas, Jürgen, 95, 101, 102–3, 114, 118, 134

Hart, H. L. A., 65

Havel, Vaclav, 119

Hebrew Bible, 121

Hegel, Georg Wilhelm Friedrich, 47

Heidegger, Martin, 39, 62, 103, 104

Henry, Michel, 66

hermeneutics, 100–109; analytical philosophy and, 96; biblical, 121; development from interpretation of symbols to interpretation of text-like works, 39; in Freud, 28; hermeneutic phenomenology, 103–4, 124; hermeneutic turn in Ricoeur, 24; and philosophy, 108–9; as reopening the closed world of texts, 108; of the self, 50, 74–76, 96; structuralism and, 39–40; of texts and of the law, 115

Hesse, Mary, 106

history, 46, 47, 106, 134

History and Truth (Histoire et vérité; Ricoeur), 22

human action. *See* action

Hume, David, 112, 132

Husserl, Edmund: bracketing, 103; and empiricism, 132; foundationalism of, 75, 96, 99; hermeneutics and structuralism as successors to, 39; idealistic phenomenology of, 17, 75, 104; influence on Ricoeur's early method, 17, 124; Ricoeur's

translation of *Ideen I*, 10, 16, 17, 75, 103; on time, 47, 111
Husserl Archives, 44, 54, 103

Ideen I (Husserl), 10, 16, 17, 75, 103
identity. *See* narrative identity; personal identity
ideology, 49
Ikor, Roger, 9, 11, 12, 16, 59, 66
institutions, 88–89, 90, 92, 128
intention, 80–81
interpretation, 100, 101, 102, 104–6
ipséité (selfhood), 67, 76, 83–86, 93, 96, 113

Jaspers, Karl, 9, 15–16, 122, 123–24
John Paul II, Pope, 46
judicial reasoning, 77
justice: ambiguity of, 90; distributive, 89, 90, 98; as fairness, 91; friendship contrasted with, 87; just inequalities, 134; and the law, 115; proportional, 92, 119; Rawls on, 90–91, 119; two sides of, 88
Justice (Ricoeur), 51

Kant, Immanuel: attempt to purify moral arguments, 95; categorical imperative, 90, 93, 114; deontological ethics of, 50, 86, 88; on personal identity, 112; putting respect for law above respect for persons, 98; on time, 47; universality in, 89, 91, 93, 94
Karl Jaspers et la philosophie de l'existence (Ricoeur and Dufrenne), 15–16
Kearney, Richard, 55–56, 67, 117
keeping a promise, 84, 93, 113
Kenny, Anthony, 65
Kermode, Frank, 121

Lacan, Jacques, 25–27, 29–31, 48, 55, 60, 70–71
Lacocque, André and Claire, 42, 63, 64
LaFitte, Sophie, 33
language: about action, 75; creativity in, 41, 45; metaphor, 41, 42–43, 106–7; "mirror of nature" problem, 106; multitude of functions of, 134–35; operations of individualization in, 78–79; poetic language, 106, 134; reference, 43, 96, 107; religious language, 41, 134; speech acts, 50, 75, 79; symbolic language, 23–24, 26
Larivaille, Paul, 71
law, 115
Lesort, Paul-André, 9, 10
Levinas, Emmanuel, 98, 110, 120
Levi-Strauss, Claude, 39, 40
literary criticism, 77

literature, 85, 108
lived body (*corps propre*), 18, 82
Locke, John, 112
love, 120, 135

Marcel, Gabriel: and dualism, 18; "Friday Afternoons," 17; influence on Ricoeur, 6, 9; Ricoeur's study of, 16
Marcellin, Raymond, 36, 57
Marrou, Henri, 21
Marx, Karl, 27, 75, 105
mêmeté (sameness), 76, 83–86, 93, 96, 113
Merleau-Ponty, Maurice, 17, 18, 26, 122, 124
metaphor, 41, 42–43, 106–7
"Metaphor and the Main Problem of Hermeneutics" ("La métaphore et le problème central de l'herméneutique"; Ricoeur), 42
Métaphore vive, La (*The Rule of Metaphor*; Ricoeur), 43–44, 65, 106, 121, 125
Miller, Jacques-Alain, 60, 70
mimesis, 47, 76
"mirror of nature" problem, 106
"Model of the Text, The: Meaningful Action Considered as a Text" (Ricoeur), 45, 49, 77
morals, 86–96; the ethical distinguished from the moral, 86; moral imputation of an action to an agent, 82; norms, 86, 91; Ricoeur's metaphysic of, 50. *See also* ethics
Mounier, Emmanuel, 19–20, 21, 59
Mounier, Paulette, 68

narration, 76, 83, 85, 111–12, 118, 119
narrative: and action, 19, 76, 119; description distinguished from, 85; in history, 47; as redescribing the world, 106–7; Ricoeur's Paris seminar on, 44–45; time and, 46, 114–15
narrative identity, 83–86; action and, 76; personal identity and, 83, 112–13
"Narrative Time" (Ricoeur), 46
natural sciences, 101, 102
Nietzsche, Friedrich: on the *cogito* as illusion, 74, 76, 96; on conscience, 98; as master of suspicion, 27, 75, 105; nihilism and skepticism of, 99; on personal identity, 112; Ricoeur's POW camp lecture on, 10
norms, 86, 91

OAS, 25
obligation, 86, 89–90, 91–92, 115
Oneself as Another (*Soi-même comme un autre*; Ricoeur), 49–50, 67, 74, 99, 118, 125

ontology of the self, 96–99
otherness, 74, 76, 88, 94–95, 97–99

Parfit, Derek, 121
"parole est mon royaume, La" (Ricoeur), 22
passivity, 97–98, 120
performatives, 79
personal identity, 78–79; narrative identity and, 83,
    112–13; in *Oneself as Another*, 50, 74, 76; as
    theme of Gifford Lectures, 48
personalism, 19
phenomenology: bracketing, 103; eidetic method, 17,
    18, 124; existential phenomenology, 121; Hei-
    degger, 39, 62, 103, 104; hermeneutic phenome-
    nology, 103–4, 124; intuitionist claims in, 100;
    Merleau-Ponty, 17, 18, 26, 122, 124; psychoanal-
    ysis contrasted with, 28; reaction against in
    France, 29; Ricoeur as proponent of, 10; Ri-
    coeur's approach to, 17, 24; Ricoeur's first paper
    on, 7; Sartre, 17–18, 22, 122; structuralism con-
    trasted with, 27, 39–40. *See also* Husserl,
    Edmund
Phenomenology of Perception (Merleau-Ponty), 17
Philip, André, 14, 15
philosophical anthropology, 19, 49, 118
philosophy: deconstructionism, 55–56, 110; develop-
    ments in France, 110; dialectics, 99; existential-
    ism, 110, 122; and hermeneutics, 108–9; as inde-
    pendent of religion, 120, 125; Ricoeur's early
    attitude toward, 5; Ricoeur's fundamental philo-
    sophical thesis, 74. *See also* analytical philoso-
    phy; ethics; phenomenology
Philosophy of the Will (Ricoeur), 17–18, 20. *See also*
    *Finitude and Culpability; Freedom and Nature:
    The Voluntary and the Involuntary*
poetic language, 106, 134
poetics, 111–12, 122, 124–25
politics: democracy, 93; ethics and, 118–19; political
    violence, 90, 113
power-in-common, 90
power to act, 82, 90
practical wisdom, 50, 92, 95, 99
precedents, legal, 115
prescription, 76, 83, 85, 107, 118, 119
promises, 84, 93, 113
pronouns, 78
proper names, 78, 80
proportional justice, 92, 119
psychoanalysis, 27–29, 40

Rawls, John, 51, 65, 88, 118, 119, 134
reading, 108

reference, 43, 96, 107
Réflections accomplies (Ricoeur), 51
religion, 78, 119–20, 125–26
"Religion, Atheism, and Faith" (Ricoeur), 40
religious language, 41, 134
Rémond, René, 34, 35, 36, 37, 38, 57–58, 131
Ricoeur, Adèle (aunt), 4, 14, 20, 61
Ricoeur, Alice (sister), 4, 5, 6, 61
Ricoeur, Etienne (son), 20, 55, 58–59, 64
Ricoeur, Florentine Favre (mother), 4, 72
Ricoeur, Jean-Paul (son), 4, 27, 55, 60
Ricoeur, Jules (father), 4, 61, 71, 126, 127
Ricoeur, Louis (grandfather), 4, 61
Ricoeur, Marc (son), 4, 54, 65
Ricoeur, Marie (grandmother), 4, 61
Ricoeur, Noëlle (daughter), 8, 14, 55, 70
Ricoeur, Olivier (son): birth of, 15; drug use, 64;
    friendship with Reagan, 54, 55; Gifford Lec-
    tures transcribed by, 48, 65; suicide of, 2, 49,
    64, 65 "Tragic Action" dedicated to, 2, 64, 92
Ricoeur, Paul (Jean Paul Gustave Ricoeur): Acadé-
    mie Française prize in philosophy, 51, 69; on Al-
    geria, 24–25, 127; the American years, 41–48;
    at Arnswald camp, 12–13; arrest during Alge-
    rian crisis, 24–25; captured by the Germans, 8;
    Christian socialism of, 6, 19, 126; at Collège
    Cévenol, 15; Croix de Guerre awarded to, 8,
    57; at "Décade de Paul Ricoeur," 66–68, 115–
    16, 117–18; as director of Husserl Archives,
    44, 103; doctorate granted to, 19; as doyen at
    Nanterre, 34–39, 57–59, 128, 129–31; driving
    of, 61; early writings, 6–7; early years, 4–7; fif-
    tieth wedding anniversary, 48; first trip to
    United States, 20; French television program
    on, 68–69; on French university system, 22–23,
    31–32, 129–30; fundamental philosophical the-
    sis of, 74; future projects of, 134–35; Gifford
    Lectures, 48–49, 65, 74, 112–14, 118; at Gross
    Born camp, 8–12; at Haverford College, 20,
    128; Hegel Prize awarded to, 69; honorary doc-
    torates granted to, 42, 71, 132; at Institute of Eu-
    ropean studies, 52–53, 60; international confer-
    ence on, 63; in Japan, 44; and Lacan, 26–27,
    30–31, 55, 70–71; liberation of, 14; living at
    Les Murs Blancs, 21; marriage, 6; military ser-
    vice, 6, 56; mobilization of, 7; in Munich in
    1939, 7; at Nanterre, 31–41, 44–45, 69, 71, 128,
    129–31; at National Center for the Humanities,
    63–64; and 1968 events, 33–34; as pacifist, 2, 7,
    10, 57, 59, 126–28; and philosophy, 5; planned
    trilogy, 123–25; during the postwar years,
    14–21; as prisoner of war, 2, 8–14, 66; POW

camp journals, 10, 16, 66; Protestant upbringing of, 4, 125; return to France, 48–51; at the Sorbonne, 5–6, 21–31; summer vacations at Préfailles, 6, 20, 51, 61–62; teaching in St. Brieuc, 5; Terry Lectures, 26; translation of Husserl, 10, 16, 17, 75, 103; at University of Chicago, 39, 41, 45, 73, 131–33; at University of Louvain, 39, 41, 131; at University of Rennes, 5; at University of Strasbourg, 16–17; and the university within the camp, 10, 12; during the war years, 7–14, 57; writing style of, 133; Zaharoff Lecture, 44

Ricoeur, Simone Lejas (wife): in Chicago, 41, 42; fiftieth wedding anniversary, 48; illness of, 68, 70; marriage, 6; meets Ricoeur, 4; during mobilization year, 7; during Ricoeur's captivity, 8; as source for this biography, 56, 61

rights, 87, 95, 115

Rorty, Richard, 106, 107

Roudinesco, Elisabeth, 30–31, 70

Rule of Metaphor, The (*La Métaphore vive;* Ricoeur), 43–44, 65, 106, 121, 125

Russell, Bertrand, 122, 132

Ryle, Gilbert, 132

sameness (*mêmeté*), 76, 83–86, 93, 96, 113

Sartre, Jean-Paul, 17–18, 22, 122

Schleiermacher, Friedrich, 104

sciences: natural, 101, 102; social, 77

Searle, John R., 79

self, the: the *cogito*, 74–75, 76, 96; ethical dimension of, 86–96; hermeneutics of, 50, 74–77, 96; as a moral being, 50; ontology of the, 96–99. *See also* personal identity

self-esteem, 86–87, 88, 98

selfhood (*ipséité*), 67, 76, 83–86, 93, 96, 113

self-respect, 86

Semantics of Action, The (*La Sémantique de l'action;* Ricoeur), 41

similitude, 88

situation-limite, 16

social contract, 90, 91

socialism, Christian, 6, 19, 126

social sciences, 77

Soi-même comme un autre (*Oneself as Another;* Ricoeur), 49–50, 67, 74, 99, 118, 125

solicitude, 87, 88, 89, 90, 93, 94

Sophocles, 92

Spanish Civil War, 127

speech acts, 50, 75, 79

Stewart, David and Audrey, 65

Strawson, P. F., 79, 81, 82, 96, 97

structuralism, 27, 39–40, 48, 96, 110, 122

"Structure, Word, and Event" ("La Structure, le mot, et l'événement"; Ricoeur), 40

suffering: and acting, 64, 76, 85, 88, 113, 135; in Ricoeur's projects for the future, 120, 123, 135

superego, 99

suspicion, 27, 75, 97, 98, 105

symbolic language, 23–24, 26

Symbolism of Evil, The (Ricoeur), 23–24, 25, 26, 40

"Technique and Nontechnique in Interpretation" ("Technique et non-technique dans l'interprétation"; Ricoeur), 40

teleology, 50, 86, 89, 91, 95

Terry Lectures, 26

Tillich, Paul, 132

time: antinomies of, 111–12: lyrical aspect of, 114; narrative and, 46, 114–15; personality identity and, 83–84; Ricoeur's Institute for European Studies course on, 52; as theme of Ricoeur, 45, 47

Time and Narrative (Ricoeur), 47–48, 110–12; and the aporia of temporality, 114; articles preparatory to, 46; exciting renewed interest in Ricoeur, 73; *From Text to Action* and, 65; and other philosophers, 60; and Ricoeur's planned trilogy, 125

"To Make the University" ("Faire l'Université"; Ricoeur), 31

tragedy of action, 92, 94

Trocmé, André and Magda, 14

universality, 89, 91, 93, 94, 95

utopia, 49

Valabréga, J.-P., 30, 68

Van der Leeuw, Gerardus, 29

verbs, 78

victimization, 113, 114

violence, 90, 99, 113

Volontaire et l'involontaire, Le. See *Freedom and Nature: The Voluntary and the Involuntary*

Wahl, François, 47, 60, 120

Wahl, Jean, 52

will, the, 18–19, 89, 124

Winock, Michel, 55, 64

Wittgenstein, Ludwig, 134

world, the: metaphor and narrative redescribing, 106–7; of the text, 107–8

Zaharoff Lecture, 44